Llewellyn's

D1608769

Witches' Datebook

2015

Featuring

Art by Kathleen Edwards
Text by Elizabeth Barrette, Deborah Blake,
Dallas Jennifer Cobb, Sybil Fogg,
Magenta Griffith, Melanie Marquis, Diana Rajchel,
Suzanne Ress, and Tess Whitehurst

ISBN 978-0-7387-2691-5

2015

	JANUARY					
S	M	T	W	T	F	S
				1	2	3
4	5	6	7	8	9	10
11	12	13	14	15	16	17
18	19	20	21	22	23	24
25	26	27	28	29	30	31

	FEBRUARY					
S	M	T	W	T	F	S
1	2	3	4	5	6	7
8	9	10	11	12	13	14
15	16	17	18	19	20	21
22	23	24	25	26	27	28

	MARCH					
S	M	T	W	T	F	S
1	2	3	4	5	6	7
8	9	10	11	12	13	14
15	16	17	18	19	20	21
22	23	24	25	26	27	28
29	30	31				

	APRIL					
S	M	T	W	T	F	S
			1	2	3	4
5	6	7	8	9	10	11
12	13	14	15	16	17	18
19	20	21	22	23	24	25
26	27	28	29	30		

	MAY					
S	M	T	W	T	F	S
					1	2
3	4	5	6	7	8	9
10	11	12	13	14	15	16
17	18	19	20	21	22	23
24	25	26	27	28	29	30
31						

	JUNE					
S	M	T	W	T	F	S
	1	2	3	4	5	6
7	8	9	10	11	12	13
14	15	16	17	18	19	20
21	22	23	24	25	26	27
28	29	30				

	JULY					
S	M	T	W	T	F	S
			1	2	3	4
5	6	7	8	9	10	11
12	13	14	15	16	17	18
19	20	21	22	23	24	25
26	27	28	29	30	31	

	AUGUST					
S	M	T	W	T	F	S
						1
2	3	4	5	6	7	8
9	10	11	12	13	14	15
16	17	18	19	20	21	22
23	24	25	26	27	28	29
30	31					

	SEPTEMBER					
S	M	T	W	T	F	S
		1	2	3	4	5
6	7	8	9	10	11	12
13	14	15	16	17	18	19
20	21	22	23	24	25	26
27	28	29	30			

	OCTOBER					
S	M	T	W	T	F	S
				1	2	3
4	5	6	7	8	9	10
11	12	13	14	15	16	17
18	19	20	21	22	23	24
25	26	27	28	29	30	31

	NOVEMBER					
S	M	T	W	T	F	S
1	2	3	4	5	6	7
8	9	10	11	12	13	14
15	16	17	18	19	20	21
22	23	24	25	26	27	28
29	30					

	DECEMBER					
S	M	T	W	T	F	S
		1	2	3	4	5
6	7	8	9	10	11	12
13	14	15	16	17	18	19
20	21	22	23	24	25	26
27	28	29	30	31		

2016

	JANUARY					
S	M	T	W	T	F	S
					1	2
3	4	5	6	7	8	9
10	11	12	13	14	15	16
17	18	19	20	21	22	23
24	25	26	27	28	29	30
31						

	FEBRUARY					
S	M	T	W	T	F	S
	1	2	3	4	5	6
7	8	9	10	11	12	13
14	15	16	17	18	19	20
21	22	23	24	25	26	27
28	29					

	MARCH					
S	M	T	W	T	F	S
		1	2	3	4	5
6	7	8	9	10	11	12
13	14	15	16	17	18	19
20	21	22	23	24	25	26
27	28	29	30	31		

	APRIL					
S	M	T	W	T	F	S
					1	2
3	4	5	6	7	8	9
10	11	12	13	14	15	16
17	18	19	20	21	22	23
24	25	26	27	28	29	30

	MAY					
S	M	T	W	T	F	S
1	2	3	4	5	6	7
8	9	10	11	12	13	14
15	16	17	18	19	20	21
22	23	24	25	26	27	28
29	30	31				

	JUNE					
S	M	T	W	T	F	S
			1	2	3	4
5	6	7	8	9	10	11
12	13	14	15	16	17	18
19	20	21	22	23	24	25
26	27	28	29	30		

	JULY					
S	M	T	W	T	F	S
					1	2
3	4	5	6	7	8	9
10	11	12	13	14	15	16
17	18	19	20	21	22	23
24	25	26	27	28	29	30
31						

	AUGUST					
S	M	T	W	T	F	S
	1	2	3	4	5	6
7	8	9	10	11	12	13
14	15	16	17	18	19	20
21	22	23	24	25	26	27
28	29	30	31			

	SEPTEMBER					
S	M	T	W	T	F	S
				1	2	3
4	5	6	7	8	9	10
11	12	13	14	15	16	17
18	19	20	21	22	23	24
25	26	27	28	29	30	

	OCTOBER					
S	M	T	W	T	F	S
						1
2	3	4	5	6	7	8
9	10	11	12	13	14	15
16	17	18	19	20	21	22
23	24	25	26	27	28	29
30	31					

	NOVEMBER					
S	M	T	W	T	F	S
		1	2	3	4	5
6	7	8	9	10	11	12
13	14	15	16	17	18	19
20	21	22	23	24	25	26
27	28	29	30			

	DECEMBER					
S	M	T	W	T	F	S
				1	2	3
4	5	6	7	8	9	10
11	12	13	14	15	16	17
18	19	20	21	22	23	24
25	26	27	28	29	30	31

Editing/design by Ed Day

Cover illustration and interior art © 2014 by Kathleen Edwards

Art on chapter openings © 2006 by Jennifer Hewitson

Art direction by Lynne Menturweck

Table of Contents

How to Use *Llewellyn's Witches' Datebook* 4

Play Day Magick *by Melanie Marquis* 6

Automatic Writing *by Sybil Fogg* 10

Relaxation NOW *by Elizabeth Barrette* 14

Seduction Magick *by Suzanne Ress* 19

Moon Mayhem *by Dallas Jennifer Cobb* 24

January 28

February 37

March 45

April 54

May 62

June 72

July 80

August 89

September 98

October 106

November 115

December 124

About the Authors 134

Appendix 136

Notes 142

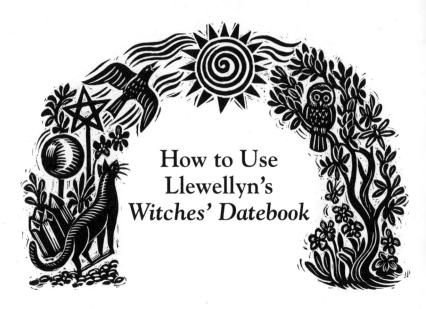

How to Use Llewellyn's *Witches' Datebook*

Welcome to *Llewellyn's Witches' Datebook 2015*! This datebook was designed especially for Witches, Pagans, and magical people. Use it to plan sabbat celebrations, magic, Full Moon rites, and even dentist and doctor appointments. At right is a symbol key to some of the features of this datebook.

MOON QUARTERS: The Moon's cycle is divided into four quarters, which are noted in the calendar pages along with their exact times. When the Moon changes quarter, both quarters are listed, as well as the time of the change. In addition, a symbol for the new quarter is placed where the numeral for the date usually appears.

MOON IN THE SIGNS: Approximately every two and a half days, the Moon moves from one zodiac sign to the next. The sign that the Moon is in at the beginning of the day (midnight Eastern Time) is noted next to the quarter listing. If the Moon changes signs that day, there will be a notation saying "☽ enters" followed by the symbol for the sign it is entering.

MOON VOID-OF-COURSE: Just before the Moon enters a new sign, it will make one final aspect (angular relationship) to another planet. Between that last aspect and the entrance of the Moon into the next sign it is said to be void-of-course. Activities begun when the Moon is void-of-course rarely come to fruition, or they turn out very differently than planned.

PLANETARY MOVEMENT: When a planet or asteroid moves from one sign into another, this change (called an *ingress*) is noted on the calendar pages with the exact time. The Moon and Sun are considered planets in this case. The planets (except for the Sun and Moon) can also appear to move backward as seen from the Earth. This is called a *planetary retrograde,* and is noted on the calendar pages with the symbol ℞. When the planet begins to move forward, or direct, again, it is marked D, and the time is also noted.

PLANTING AND HARVESTING DAYS: The best days for planting and harvesting are noted on the calendar pages with a seedling icon (planting) and a basket icon (harvesting).

TIME ZONE CHANGES: The times and dates of all astrological phenomena in this datebook are based on Eastern time. If you live outside the Eastern time zone, you will need to make the following changes: Pacific Time subtract three hours; Mountain Time subtract two hours; Central Time subtract one hour; Alaska subtract four hours; and Hawaii subtract five hours. All data is adjusted for Daylight Saving Time.

Planets

☉	Sun	♆	Neptune
☽	Moon	♇	Pluto
☿	Mercury	⚷	Chiron
♀	Venus	⚳	Ceres
♂	Mars	⚴	Pallas
♃	Jupiter	⚵	Juno
♄	Saturn	⚶	Vesta
♅	Uranus		

Signs

♈	Aries	♐	Sagittarius
♉	Taurus	♑	Capricorn
♊	Gemini	♒	Aquarius
♋	Cancer	♓	Pisces
♌	Leo		
♍	Virgo		**Motion**
♎	Libra	℞	Retrograde
♏	Scorpio	D	Direct

1st Quarter/New Moon ☽   3rd Quarter/Full Moon ☺
2nd Quarter ☽   4th Quarter ☽

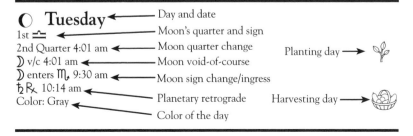

Play Day Magick
by Melanie Marquis

Childhood is a time of preparation, readying us not just for adulthood, but also for a life of magick. While certainly not the only medium for education, play is indeed important. Our childhood experiences of play—or in many cases, sadly, a lack of such experiences, can have a strong bearing on our general effectiveness as adults as well as on our overall magickal prowess.

Through play, we learn about life in the mundane world, and we also come to master the skills and abilities needed for success in the arts of magick. If you were able to enjoy a lot of worry-free play as a child, chances are you cultivated the imagination, curiosity, and creativity needed to make you a natural at magick. If opportunities for childhood play were scant due to unfortunate circumstances, one typically develops great skill at escapism, another ability that comes in handy for spellwork. Imagination takes us away from where we are or what we're going through, and when it's used in this way as a tool for survival and healing, it often develops a more tangible quality that transfers into greater magickal power and potential.

Whether or not you played often as a child, it's never too late for more fun. Combining play and magick by putting a new twist on childhood toys, games, and other kid stuff is a great way to relieve stress, gain confidence, and improve your effectiveness as both a world citizen and a witch. If you'd like to try some play magick, here are a few activities. Try these with an open mind and a playful attitude for best results!

Spinning Top Charm

A simple spinning top can be used effectively for magick intended to speed something up or slow something down. Hold the top in your hand and think about the circumstance you're aiming to affect, infusing the top with this new identity. For instance, if you wanted to speed up the processing of a job application, you would think about the top as if it is the actual job application itself. As another example, if you wanted to impede the spread of weeds in your garden, you would think about the top as being the weeds, empowering it to be a perfect stand-in and substitute for the actual weeds it represents.

Spin the top. If you're looking to speed something up, spin it as fast as you can, and think about the circumstance you want to affect speeding up, moving more swiftly by the second as the top rotates. If you like, incorporate a chant such as, "Fast, faster, fastest!" to help magnify the magickal power.

End the visualization and cast the energy of your intentions into the top while it is still spinning strongly; look away and end the spell before spinning slows. If you don't get it right on your first shot—just try again until you do. Alternatively, if you were trying to slow something down, you would spin the top and then impede it, perhaps nudging it with your wand to give it a clumsy rotation, or stopping it abruptly mid-spin with a tap of your fingertip, beginning visualizations as the top loses its speed and casting the core of the magick at the moment the top stops completely.

Stuffed Animal Magick

Stuffed animals aren't just cute and cuddly; they also provide a fun way to enjoy making more magick with our personal spirit animals and totems. In fact, stuffed ani-

mals make a wonderful medium for working with the energies of all sorts of animals, be they spirit animals, totemic animals, actual animals, or even fantastic, make-believe animals.

Empower the stuffed animal with the energy and spirit of the animal it is to represent. For instance, if you have a teddy bear you want to use to work with the

Grizzly Bear totem, fill the stuffed animal with strong, wild energy, inviting the spirit of the real grizzly to actually enter cloth bear. Once the stuffed animal has been readied for magick, you can use it in a variety of ways. Simply hug or stroke the animal to charge yourself with the qualities therein embodied, or place the stuffed animal on your altar for extra help and power during spellcasting. You might even empower the stuffed animal to represent an animal that needs protection, then use it as a focal point for casting protective charms and spells. For instance, you might place a stuffed elephant outside in the grass, then set up a large perimeter of protective crystals around it as a way to help magickally manifest a safe sanctuary for these precious endangered creatures. As another idea, if you wanted to use a stuffed animal to get more in touch with your own personal spirit animal, you might choose a stuffed animal that best represents you, then dress it in clothes to make it resemble you, or simply write your name on its tag or on its fur. Play like you're taking good care of this animal, feeding it and loving it and making sure it gets plenty of rest and such. Nurturing your stuffed animal-made-spirit animal will increase the intimacy between you and your inner beast.

Jigsaw Puzzle Spell

Putting together a jigsaw puzzle can easily be transformed into a powerful act of magick. By finding the right pieces and putting them in all the right places, a new and perfect picture is formed, a formula that happens to be perfectly suited for magick intended to help you overcome challenges and gather resources needed for success.

You have several puzzle options to choose from for this type of spellwork. The simplest is a ready-made cardboard puzzle with an image you can use to represent your magickal goal. For example, a puzzle depicting a beautiful bouquet of roses could symbolize the lovely hopes you want to achieve, while a puzzle depicting a formidable stone castle might be used to represent the stable foundation on which you hope to build your dreams. If you can't find a puzzle that seems suitable, one option is to order a custom-made design from a company that converts photos or drawings into jigsaw puzzles. Depending on size and quality, custom-made puzzles can range in price from an average of $5.00 to around $25.00. If you'd rather keep costs minimal, pick up a cheap puzzle from the dollar store and paint it yourself to perfectly suit your spell goal. Just be sure to use tempura paint, which dries quickly, and use a thin coat so that the pieces won't be impossible to separate once the paint dries.

Lay the pieces in front of you. As you turn them all face up, imagine that you're revealing all the elements needed to make your dreams come true. Begin assembling the puzzle's border, envisioning as you do so that you are creating a space in which your wishes can manifest. Proceed by filling in the rest of the puzzle, imagining each piece you place as another skill, resource, or opportunity that will help you achieve your goal. Once the puzzle is complete, affirm through visualization or words that your magickal wishes are now manifest.

Magickal Hide-and-Go-Seek

Need an opportunity or a resource to manifest? Grab a friend and try a round of magickal hide-and-go-seek! One person acts as the seeker, while the other person becomes an embodiment of whatever is desired, be it a new car, more food, a job, a peaceful environment, or any other goal. The hider hides, then the seeker finds, shouting at the moment their quarry is first sighted that they have definitely found exactly what they were looking for, exactly what they need.

More Magickal Fun

The ideas in this article are a very small sampling of all the possibilities for play magick, which are endless! Let your own childhood playtime favorites inspire you to devise even more types of magickal fun. Might you be able to skip over obstacles by skipping an enchanted jump rope? Could a game of magickal freeze tag be used to stop fear, doubt, or other baneful energies? Perhaps those dolls or action figures could come in handy for a bit of imitative magick, allowing you to mimic and play act the circumstances you desire. Challenge yourself to come up with some new ideas for play magick. How might you use a bouncy ball as a tool for magick? Could imaginative play fighting, make-believe caregiving, or other forms of role-play be of magickal benefit? What other ideas can you think of? Play and magick are intrinsically linked, and the potential, possibility, and power of play magick are truly as limitless as the value of fun itself!

Automatic Writing

by Sybil Fogg

Automatic writing is a form of divination in which a medium holds a pen or pencil (or lays their fingers over the keyboard) and allows for their subconscious or an otherworldly messenger to take control and write. Throughout history, people have attested to having used this exercise to write short to lengthy works (even novels). Those who have succeeded in drawing words this way, state that the act of writing comes from the deep subconscious state, spirit world, or other external source without the writer's conscious awareness of the content. Automatic writing holds its place amongst other forms of communicating with the spirits, such as talking boards, scrying, casting runes, and/or tarot readings.

Although many people have claimed art was created via automatic writing, one of the most famous is the Irish poet, William Butler Yeats, who credited much of his later writings to information gleaned from his wife's, Georgie Hyde-Lees, automatic writing. It can probably be stated that Hyde-Lees's mystical talent cemented their marriage. Over time, there has been speculation that her gift was fabricated to keep Yeats's attention on herself and away from his long-term desire for the Irish revolutionary, Maud Gonne MacBride.

Automatic writing allows us to seek guidance by accessing our deeper selves or spiritual entities. It might even assist in recalling locked or suppressed memories or help us to connect with a mystical energy to promote self-revelation and personal growth.

When practicing automatic writing, it is best to have a working question. As in most magical practices, this question should be posed in a way that allows for an open flow of communication. A yes or no query will not work with automatic writing. This does not allow time to fully tap the resources available and will not produce the kind of results we generally look for in this exercise. For example: "Will I ever find true love?" will not draw as full an experience as "How can I draw loving energy to me?"

When first trying this type of fortune-telling, practitioners may find that they end up with a series of dashes and lines and no real letters or words. This is normal, as the body and mind become attuned to the spirit world around us. Or perhaps like the nineteenth-century medium Hélène Smith (who claimed that she did automatic writing to convey messages from Mars in Martian language), it is another language or being that is picked up in the automatic writing. You may find that you need to do a dozen or so sittings before you start really getting answers to your questions or feeling that you have connected to another being.

There is no real need to organize a ritual around automatic writing, but I find that I can enter a deeper trance when I have prepared a space, called the quarters, cast a circle, and drawn down the Goddess. Because these small flourishes put me in a more relaxed place mentally and emotionally, I have had far more success with automatic writing than when I just sit down and start writing. To bookend the process, at the end of the session I always put out an offering of thanks.

Enhancing magic through any type of divination is a possibility, and the following ritual is designed to bring automatic writing into our magical workings. Like other rituals, focus is necessary and this exercise will fall apart quickly with distractions, so make sure to carve out a lengthy period of solitude to work this spell. I find late nights when the household is most assuredly asleep to be the best time, but we each have our own personal situations. So make sure to spend some time planning.

Automatic Writing Ritual – Tools Needed

Writing utensil and paper

Yellow spell candle (spell candles are small thin tapers that will burn down within the time frame of a ritual) anointed with ambergris to prepare for a psychic journey.

Incense: Use a combination of clove to activate the dark corners of memory, myrrh to ease into a meditative state, and frankincense to unlock the spiritual plane.

Candles for the four quarters

Cakes and ale (or another type of offering) for the Goddess and God.

Pillows or cushions because it can be difficult to kneel or sit on the floor for an extended period of time. If you are not comfortable, it will be hard to truly release yourself to the ritual.

Anything else you feel is necessary to enhance success. I often put together a mini altar with a small wooden table covered by an altar cloth, with icons of the God and Goddess along, and completed with any trinkets I feel will aid in the spiritual quest.

Preparation: In the days before you actualize this ritual, plan your question(s). You may want to call upon a certain deity or spirit, so make sure you do any necessary research. For example, in matters of love you might decide to invoke Aphrodite, Radhe Krishna, or Eros. Or maybe all of them. This will also help determine an offering. Apples for Aphrodite, ladoos for Radhe Krishna, or dark chocolate for Eros.

Before partaking in any magical acts, it is best to take a ritual cleansing bath to purify yourself and prepare mentally for the automatic writing.

Set up your space. If using, place the altar in the middle and scatter the pillows around it.

Put out the offering for the God and Goddess.

Place your writing paraphernalia where you will be comfortable.

Set the candle in the middle of the altar (or designated space).

Set out and light the incense.

Conducting the Ritual

Time: This ritual is best performed on a Wednesday evening during a waning moon in Scorpio.

Call the quarters and cast the circle as you normally do.

Get comfortable with your writing tools and face the yellow candle. Meditate for a moment or do some deep breathing exercises.

Light the yellow candle and pose your question. You may choose to invoke a specific god or goddess for this part. In fact, you can write to them in your first line.

Once you have your question down, start writing and don't worry or even think about what you are writing. Just let the pen move across the paper, letting it flow. You might find that you are not even making words or letters. This does

not matter. Simply keep going. Don't stop. Don't worry about how much time you are dedicating to the writing, just flow. Don't worry about spelling or grammatical errors. Don't expect complete sentences or thoughts. This exercise is not about formal writing. With more practice, you will find yourself writing longer passages, but for now it will feel strange or even silly, but keep at it. Eventually you will feel a release and your mind will feel blank. Keep writing.

The goal is to write until the yellow candle has burned down. If you find that you keep stopping, seeing the candle, and picking up the pen again, don't fret. This is perfectly natural in your first few sittings. Write until you cannot anymore and then spend the rest of the candle's flickering duration meditating on your question and the process.

Alternatively, if you are still writing and the candle has burnt out, keep going until you feel spent.

Once you have completed the ritual, thank the Goddess and God, quarters, and close the circle.

You might feel physically drained after a session. This is normal as you have been a conduit. Once the ritual is completed, be sure to take care of yourself. Do some gentle stretches to work out any stiff muscles, replenish with fluids, eat something, and get a good night's sleep.

If you have enjoyed this exercise, work into a regular activity. Feel free to play around with the correspondences. Base them on the questions posed. This might very well change the timing, incense, and anointments. Automatic writing has its place in each of our personal journeys and spiritual development. With practice blended with ritual, we can utilize this means of divination to tap into our deepest selves or touch the mystical realm around us.

Relaxation NOW!
by Elizabeth Barrette

In today's stressful world, it can be difficult to find time to release the tension that builds up during the day. This article focuses on methods that you can use anywhere and/or that make use of time you've already blocked out for another necessary activity. They don't require you to set aside a whole separate place or time just to unwind.

Relaxation offers many benefits. It slows and deepens your breathing. It slows your heartbeat and lowers blood pressure. It improves blood flow to your muscles and releases tension, which can relieve some types of pain. Your concentration increases, which also boosts your ability to solve problems. Anger, frustration, and negative emotions decrease. While relaxed, you are better prepared to handle whatever challenges you encounter.

Breathing Exercises

Because we are always breathing, this relaxation technique may be done anywhere, anytime. It is quite discreet and requires no extra equipment. It also works especially well for feelings of anxiety or panic. The goal is to slow and deepen your breaths, which encourages the rest of the body to follow into a restful state. If possible, sit with your back straight to give your chest plenty of room to expand.

Breathe from your belly. When you inhale, use your diaphragm to pull air down into your lungs, pushing your belly outward. When you exhale, your diaphragm rises back to its resting place and your belly relaxes toward your spine. If you breathe only from your chest, it's shorter and faster.

Loosen your upper body. The muscles of your face, neck, and shoulders should remain soft. Imagine the air flowing down to the bottom of your lungs. Stress tends to tighten the muscles from the chest upward, making it difficult to take a full breath.

Smooth out the rough edges. Relaxed breathing has a flow uninterrupted by hitches or huffs. Let the inhalation and exhalation move naturally from one to another, like waves rising and falling. If you snatch at your breath, it will not be as satisfying.

Take your time exhaling. If you're in a relaxed state, the exhalations will last slightly longer than the inhalations. It's important to empty the lungs as completely as possible, to make room for fresh air. Concentrate on the outflow and try to stretch it just a moment longer. Tension tends to cause short, choppy exhalations that don't let out enough stale air.

Pause between exhalation and inhalation. In a peaceful state, the body naturally rests for a moment between each breath cycle. This promotes feelings of stillness and tranquility. Under stress, the body pulls in air as fast as possible, reducing or omitting this restful pause.

Progressive Muscle Relaxation

This technique is fairly discreet and requires no extra equipment. It works best in contexts where you can sit down or lie back for a few minutes. It's especially effective for relieving stress headaches or cramps. It also relaxes the mind by relaxing the body. Pay attention to how stiff and stressed you feel before starting.

The idea is to tense and release muscle groups, going through the whole body in slow motion. Begin by curling your toes for a few seconds, then uncurling them. Next, bend your feet toward your body, hold, and let go. Clench your thighs, pressing your knees together, then relax. Tighten your hip muscles, pause, and loosen them. Firm your belly, then let it soften. Stiffen your back, hold it, and release.

Lift your shoulders toward your head, touching your ears if you can, then lower them. Tense your upper arms and relax. Tighten your forearms, clench your fists, and let go. Scrunch your face, then let it return to a neutral expression.

Move your whole body, softly, to test how different it feels from when you started. Your body should feel more limber and your mind more tranquil.

Self-Massage

This works best when you have a little privacy, such as in your car or a bathroom, or if nobody else is nearby. It's ideal for relieving stiffness and helping yourself feel loved.

Massage your shoulders by placing each hand on its own shoulder. Squeeze and rub with your whole hands. Move inward toward your neck and press again. Slowly go up the sides of the neck, pinching and rolling the muscles between thumb and fingers.

Do your scalp by spreading your hands so that only the fingertips touch your skin on either side of your head. Move in small circles as if shampooing your hair. Shift about an inch, then repeat, moving gradually over the surface of your head.

Massage one hand at a time. Use your thumb to rub and press over the surface of the palm, paying particular attention to the web between thumb and forefinger. Grasp your fingers and pull them gently away from your palm, then toward your palm. Take each finger individually and tug it sideways away from the others. Finish by stroking firmly from fingertips to wrist. Then do the other hand.

Visualization

Use this when you're stuck somewhere stressful or boring, but you don't need to pay attention at the moment. Imagine yourself somewhere else. This relaxes the body by relaxing the mind.

Begin by settling into a comfortable position. Breathe slowly. Think of a pleasant location such as a quiet forest or a beach. Paint a vivid picture in your mind of how this place looks. Hear the sounds—birds, animals, the wind, and so forth. Reach for physical sensations—

warm, cool, rough, or smooth. Imagine smells or tastes as well. Immerse yourself in the experience as deeply as possible.

Gazing Patterns

Gazing patterns include mandalas, Celtic knotwork, and other complex images that occupy attention. They can be placed on rings, pendants, keychains, T-shirts, tattoos, bookmarks, and all kinds of other things. Using them gives a sense of completion and confidence.

Choose a line—most gazing patterns have a combination of several twined together—and follow it from the beginning to the end. Focus only on tracing the path. Try to keep your speed at a slow, even pace. If you still feel frazzled after reaching the end, you can go back to the beginning and trace another line.

Mantras

A mantra is a syllable, word, or phrase that is repeated to focus on a goal. This may be done silently in company, or aloud if you have privacy. Mantras are especially helpful in drowning out negative messages that get stuck on repeat inside your head.

A simple mantra that many people already know is "OM." It sounds like "home" without the "h" on the front. Inhale slowly, and on the exhale say "OM" as long as possible. The repetition can be very soothing.

A good one for focusing on cycles is "So-Hum." On the inhale, think "So." On the exhale, say "Hum," again drawing it out. Pull in what you need, and release what you don't need.

Soothing Sounds

For this exercise you need some kind of player and suitable recordings. It's very helpful for dealing with environments that are noisy, or uncomfortably quiet and monotonous.

Listen to something pleasant. Quiet music helps slow the metabolism, especially if you choose something with a "heartbeat" rhythm. Classical music in particular supports both intellect and intuition, while having a gentle tranquilizing effect on mind and body alike.

Moving in a different direction, nature sounds also work for relaxation. You might try recordings of a calm forest, waves on the beach, rain, or wind. Popular animal sounds include the songs of birds, whales, and wolves. Some albums combine soft music and nature sounds.

Mindfulness

This is one of the few relaxation techniques safe to practice while driving, because it increases your awareness of the here-and-now. Use it when the reason for your stress is in the past, or otherwise outside your current context.

Focus on your senses one at a time. What do you see, hear, feel, smell, and taste right now? Single out individual objects or events around you. You might notice a road sign, a person's voice, the texture of your clothes, a whiff of fresh-cut grass, or the flavor of chewing gum. Be as specific as you can.

If you are moving, notice things one at a time and then shift to something else. If you are sitting still, concentrate on a single thing and notice as many details about it as you can before moving to a new one. By emphasizing what is real, present, and current you anchor your attention to keep it from drifting into distant and more upsetting topics.

Finally, bear in mind that relaxation is a skill. Like any other skill, it takes practice to learn. You will get better over time, so don't feel disappointed if it doesn't produce big results immediately. Also consider that different techniques work for different people. You might get minimal results from visualization but great results from progressive muscle relaxation, or vice versa. If the first thing or two you try doesn't work the way you want, keep exploring until you find something that suits your needs.

Seduction Magic
by Suzanne Ress

Whether you are seducing a potential sexual partner, a new business client, or a non-human property such as money, luck, health, or happiness, in magical spellwork, your goal is to capture what you desire and divert it, from its forward-leading path, toward yourself. Put in a positive way, seduction is all about enticement, luring, capturing attention, enchantment, and, especially, charming with sensual appeal.

Techniques used in erotic seduction and in seduction magic for spellcasting always, almost without exception, appeal to all six senses.

Scent: Essential oils, scented candles, personal colognes—alluring aromas are of utmost importance in any form of seduction! Imagine how a foul, rotten, or dirty smell would immediately destroy the atmosphere for sexual seduction, as well as for magic.

Sight: The use of lighting, usually low lights, firelight, or candlelight, is much more flattering and seductive than bright office or factory lights. Focusing one's inner or actual eyes on the object of desire is imperative. Visual clutter is not seductive! Focus and beauty are!

Hearing: One's vocal tone, rhythm, amplitude, word choice, as well as breathing, sighing, and other nonverbal sounds are an essential part of seduction, both erotic and magical.

Touch: A properly timed touch of a hand to a lower arm can send shivers of erotically charged energy through the seduced person. Handholding or other physical connections between coven members

during magical rites is one of the most effective ways to raise magical energy.

Taste: Sensual treats like fresh fruit and chocolate are often used in magic at the close of the ceremony, along with some shared beverage, to seal a spell. Likewise in sexual seduction, sharing a drink or light meal means more than satisfying thirst or hunger. It is a form of communion.

Intuition: Neither seduction nor magic could work without the ability to tune in intuitively to one's desired subject or object.

To Seduce Your Dream Job

On the night of the New Moon, dress becomingly in red clothing. Carve your name into a red candle and anoint it with bay laurel essential oil. In the center of a small table place the candle in a stone or ceramic holder on top of a small piece of paper upon which you have written a detailed description of your dream job. Sit in a chair at the table, with the lit candle before you. Close your eyes and visualize yourself happily employed at your dream job. Imagine every detail of what you are doing, and who you are doing it with; focus all of your attention on how you are doing your job. Keep this image in your mind for at least ten minutes, all the while breathing deeply.

Open your eyes and extinguish the candle. Slowly eat one small square of dark chocolate while waiting for the wax to cool completely. Wrap the candle in the piece of paper, rolling it toward you, and tie it with a red string or ribbon. Put the wrapped candle away in a drawer. Your dream job will come to you.

To Seduce Money

On a Sunday before noon, bathe in water scented with a few drops of basil essential oil, dry yourself and dust your skin with a mixture of talcum powder and powdered sugar. Dress in green clothing.

Standing under a threshold at noon, anoint a small iron cup or dish with a mixture of basil, ginger, mint, and sunflower oils. While massaging the oil into the metal with your hands, breathe deeply and visualize the amount of money, in the form of a check or in cash, already in your pocket or purse.

Lift and hold the iron cup above your head in both hands, fix your eyes on it, and chant slowly, four times over:

I attract money
I attract financial well-being
I attract prosperity
I attract wealth
Money comes to me
Financial well being comes to me
Prosperity comes to me
Wealth comes to me.

Wrap the cup in a square of orange fabric and put it inside a silver or ceramic bowl, in a place where it will receive the light of day. Then forget about it. Money will come to you.

Just as in sexual seduction, in magical work the implicit deal is that you have something to offer the selected person or property, therefore he, she, or it will gladly comply with your desires. In magical spells, in order to obtain the result you wish, it must be clear to the powers that be that they will somehow benefit from the exchange. It is not difficult to attract whatever you most desire if you are ready to reciprocate with your own contributions to the universal energy.

To Seduce Long-Lasting Love

Go to a graveyard on the night of the Full Moon, dressed charmingly in white. Wear just a hint of your favorite cologne. Sit down on a bench or in the grass, and, by the light of the moon and a white candle protected in a lantern, compose a love letter telling your imagined or real companion all of the wonderful qualities you appreciate and cherish in him or her. Sign your name, sprinkle the paper with fresh rose petals, honeysuckle and jasmine flowers, and fold it up toward yourself. Drink a toast—a sip of champagne from a crystal flute. Wrap the letter in a pair of clean white underpants and carry it with you, in your purse, bag or computer case, at all times, until that special someone is yours.

Seducing Improved Health

On the eve of the first day of the month, dress entirely in blue. Invite several close friends or family members to join you for an evening of storytelling around a campfire. Sit on the ground, the palms of your hands touching the earth, and initiate the storytelling with a tale of a veiled you (use an alias), in a modified, glowingly healthy, version. This other you travels from an underground sewage tunnel deep in the bowels of the grayest, saddest city imaginable, to a sunny, flower-filled field high up on a mountain with a breathtaking panorama all around. Along the way you find a magic mirror and a bottle of long-life elixir. You meet several people and animals, which help you along the way, and you have a few adventures. In your story describe all of these things, as well as how your inner feelings change from the start of the trip to its finish. Use your voice tone, amplitude, word choice, timing—to seduce your listeners and to hold their attention. Likewise, focus all of your attention on each of your friends when it's his turn to speak.

When the stories are over, everyone should hold hands in a circle and feel the healing energy of love pulse throughout the group. See this energy as a bright blue light. Afterwards, pass around a glass goblet of fresh water mixed with a little honey and cider vinegar, from which everyone should take a sip. Retire early.

Seduction of Inner Peace

On a beautiful spring day after the rains have stopped, bring a clean white towel, a pair of clean white socks, and a mixture of mint essential oil and jojoba oil to a stream. Remove your shoes, sit down by the stream, and immerse your bare feet in the stream until they become quite cold. While you are sitting there, breathe deeply, close your eyes, and listen to the sound of the moving water, the birds, the rustling leaves, whatever surrounds you. Feel the water washing over your feet and imagine it washing your entire body, taking away all of your stresses and worries. As the water flows downstream, it carries away all your troubles, leaving you clean and refreshed.

When you take your feet out of the stream, dry them carefully on the towel, massage some oil into each foot, and put on the clean white socks. Then stand up, and in a quietly confident voice, say:

I am at peace with myself. All good things are attracted to me, for I radiate peace and well-being.

Then turn and walk away. Don't look back.

Seduction is a subtle art. While you may strongly desire someone or something, you must appear to be ambiguous. You must make yourself irresistibly attractive to your subject, so that he, she, or it feels drawn to you without realizing why.

Moon Mayhem
by Dallas Jennifer Cobb

Have you ever had one of those days when no matter what, you seem to miss the mark? Days when appliances malfunction and phone messages go missing? Or days when you feel weepy and sensitive for no apparent reason?

I had a day recently when everything seemed to be working against me. The coffee filter got clogged and the pot overflowed, the cat pooped on the floor next to the litter box, and while packing my daughter's lunch I got scalded by hot soup when the thermos overflowed as I tried to put the lid on it. "Hmmm," I thought, "what's going on?"

We all have days like this, and while there are lots of reasons for missed connections, accidents, and odd encounters with people, places, and things, consider that it may be "Moon Mayhem" at work—the deep lunar influences that act upon our lives.

On the flip side of moon mayhem are the days when I awake feeling the potential of the day calling to me, run into favorite friends out of the blue, have strangers tell me things that change my mind-set, and generally live a magically charmed existence for a while. Come on, admit it, you've had these days too. These I often attribute to "Moon Magic."

Lunar Influences

Magic or mayhem, the moon exerts significant influence over all life—the ocean, earth, humans, and animals. Much is written about lunar effects on tides, crops, agricultural cycles, and weather, but less is said about how the moon deeply and profoundly affects us and the texture of our daily lives.

Knowing how lunar phases and positioning affect you specifically can help you to anticipate the effects of the moon, prepare for it, and plan your life activities in order to work with the energy, rather than feeling like you're trying to swim against its tide.

I started tracking lunar influences seventeen years ago, and while there are still great periods of time when I completely forget, I always come back to it, usually jarred into consciousness by a period of Moon Mayhem or Moon Magic. Tracking these lunar influences has enabled me to note recurring patterns and make sense of them. With practice, I am able to recognize the lunar influences that facilitate certain activities and have a better idea of what to do, and not do, at different times.

As a planet, the moon is strongly associated with our "watery" nature, influencing our emotions, instincts, and intuition. It's considered a feminine planet and as such governs the realms we often associate with women—nurture, emotion, and deep connection. The moon also influences our relationships with women, especially our mothers, and governs our often unconscious reactions to emotional stimuli.

We often experience lunar influences as "reactions" rather than "actions," influencing how we respond, react, and interact with outside influences. The moon's influence can be felt in many realms. It affects the mind, body, physical self, emotions, the unconscious, dreams, and energy level. Around us, it affects weather, agriculture, and tides; magic, clairvoyance, manifestation, healing, and protection.

My sun sign is Cancer, so my personality and primary identity is very emotional and watery. When the moon is in Cancer, the additional dose of lunar energy filtering through watery Cancer affects my feelings, instincts, and intuitions, often in an overwhelming way. Picture me weeping and laughing as I try to tell you how I am doing today.

By observing the effects of this lunar influence over time, I have learned not to undertake any big emotional conversations or activities during this time, or I am simply inviting Moon Mayhem to work on me, my emotions, and my relationships. If I am going to set a date to meet up with my mother, for example, I won't schedule it during a Cancer moon because all that energy of emotion, combined with the unconscious reactions to my mother, can make for a crazy, emotional time. I find it better to schedule visits with her during moon in Capricorn, so I can set good boundaries and focus on traditions and family responsibilities.

Knowing where the moon sits in your natal chart can provide an understanding of where you will be most sensitive, emotional, and intuitive, and can often indicate the sort of people, or energies, you will be attracted to. Use an online astrological site to determine your moon sign.

Phases, Transits, and Moon Void-of-Course

Lunar influences are ever changing because the moon is always changing phase and transiting through the signs. Knowing what phase the moon is in will enable you to understand the influence the moon is exacting at that time and better use it to enhance your life, work, and magical work. Knowing what sign it is transiting through will help you to identify the particular energy of the sign, that the moon is "illuminating."

Use specific lunar phases amplify lunar energy to support and enhance what you seek to do. Recently, given the opportunity to speak publicly to a large crowd, I worked with the organizers to choose a day that would enhance my public speaking ability and personal magnetism. Initially, I looked at the phase of the moon and chose the time between the first quarter and Full Moon, so I would be supported by growing energy. Then I looked for a day when the moon was in Leo (to support my magnetic personality and bring me public recognition) or Sagittarius (to support a new endeavor and give me help "wing it"). I went into the event feeling supported cosmically and energetically.

I have also found that when moon is considered void-of-course (the time between its last contact with any planet in the current Zodiac sign and when it enters the next sign) is a time for me to plan to do little. The moon is paused between visits to the astrological houses, so I try to pause, and not plan any big visits, undertakings, or major change.

When the moon is void-of-course lunar energy is essentially suspended, and I find myself flailing in the world. Because I have a Cancer Sun (and am governed by the moon), lots of my core energy comes from the moon, and the void-of-course times produce havoc for me. There is literally no lunar energy for me to draw on. Void-of-course produces flat emotions, little intuition, and poor mental/cognitive functioning. These are times when I try to stay close to home, sometimes just stay in bed, and focus on gentle nurture and sleep.

The Mayhem and Magic

It's easy to understand the moon's influence on your life so you can avoid moon mayhem or fully engage moon magic. Each evening, look at tomorrow in your date-book. You can both mentally pre-pare for tomorrow's appointments and responsibilities, and make note of lunar influences.Be aware of what phase the moon is in, and what sign it's transiting through.

Over time you'll develop a sense of what signs bring positive and sup-portive energy to particular areas, what signs bring chaotic energy, and what offers low or no energy.

Expand your end of the day routine to include making a note of the sort of day you had. Develop a tracking system that suits you. Maybe you're an "emoticon" kind of person and will draw little faces to indicate the emotional character of your day, or you'll use numbers to attach a ranking to the day's energy or sacred symbols that denote whether it was a day of gratitude, protection, or manifestation. The choice is yours.

Over time, the themes will emerge. Your notes will identify the magical days when synchronicity and flow are at work within and around you, when you feel energized and happy, gorgeous and magnetic. And you will note the mayhem days, when you need to work hard to stay in the present, to ground and affirm yourself, and to do the small routines and rituals that keep you in touch with your chosen reality.

You can use this knowledge to look ahead and prepare for the recur-rence of lunar influences, minimizing your struggles against the tide, and maximizing the flow of lunar energy.

Don't forget to give yourself a break. Like all magical and ener-getic work, tracking lunar influences is about practice, not perfection. Sometimes it's all I can do to get through today. If you're like me, it will be in exhaustion or frustration at the end of a particularly chal-lenging day that you'll find yourself flipping desperately through the datebook to determine the lunar influences of the day.

Relax. Make note of how you feel, and know your knowledge of lunar influences is growing, and this difficult day will help you to more purposefully engage lunar magic or mayhem consciously in your life.

29 Monday
2nd ♈
☽ v/c 7:46 pm
Color: White

30 Tuesday
2nd ♈
☽ enters ♉ 5:56 am
Color: Scarlet

31 Wednesday
2nd ♉
Color: Yellow

New Year's Eve

1 Thursday
2nd ♉
☽ v/c 7:19 am
☽ enters ♊ 12:09 pm
Color: Green

New Year's Day
Kwanzaa ends

2 Friday
2nd ♊
Color: Rose

Maha Shivaratri (India)

In India, this Full Moon is a celebration of the Hindu god Shiva, in his avatar of Nataraja, Lord of the Dance, and is considered his birthday. In Tamil areas of South India and Sri Lanka, the festival is called Arudra Darshan, in the rest of India, Maha Shivaratri. On this day, he is worshiped with chanting from the Vedas. These holidays celebrates the ecstatic dance of Lord Shiva, which represents five activities—creation,  protection, destruction, embodiment, and release—the cycle of creation and destruction. This cosmic dance takes place in every particle of being and is the source of all energy. When Shiva dances, he represents truth, and by dancing, he banishes ignorance and helps relieve the suffering of his followers. On this day, he is worshiped with chanting from Vedas.

As the longest night of Full Moon all year, this is a wonderful night for ecstatic dance ritual. Find a place where there is room to dance (by yourself or with friends). You may use recorded music or take turns drumming instead. Don't worry about making a mistake—just move to the music. Be creative and imaginative, and dance yourself into being.

—Magenta Griffith

---

3 Saturday
2nd ♊
☽ v/c 6:55 am
♀ enters ♒ 9:48 am
☽ enters ♋ 8:08 pm
Color: Black

Begin the new year as you mean to end it

☺ Sunday
2nd ♋
☿ enters ♒ 8:08 pm
☽ v/c 11:53 pm
Full Moon 11:53 pm
Color: Gold

Cold Moon

---

5 Monday

3rd ♋
Color: Ivory

6 Tuesday

3rd ♋
☽ enters ♌ 6:03 am
Color: Scarlet

Twelfth Night/Epiphany

7 Wednesday

3rd ♌
Color: Yellow

Garnet on a keychain protects during travel

8 Thursday

3rd ♌
♀ enters ♑ 10:24 am
☽ v/c 12:05 pm
☽ enters ♍ 5:58 pm
Color: Crimson

Fern leaves symbolize magic and fascination

9 Friday

3rd ♍
Color: White

10 Saturday
3rd ♍
☽ v/c 10:46 am
Color: Blue

11 Sunday
3rd ♍
☽ enters ♎ 6:57 am
Color: Yellow

*Surya mudra: fold the ring finger completely under
the thumb to raise body temperature when you feel cold*

January

12 Monday
3rd ♎
♂ enters ♓ 5:20 am
Color: Gray

Yao-shih, the Chinese god of healing, can also grant psychic powers

○ Tuesday
3rd ♎
☽ v/c 4:46 am
4th quarter 4:46 am
☽ enters ♏ 6:44 pm
Color: White

14 Wednesday
4th ♏
Color: Brown

15 Thursday
4th ♏
☽ v/c 6:52 pm
Color: Purple

Asteroid Artemis symbolizes
wildness and independence in astrology

16 Friday
4th ♏
☽ enters ♐ 3:01 am
Color: Coral

Set in Eastern Standard Time (EST)

Crocus

Crocus is famous for bursting forth and blooming when it's cold out—even through a carpet of snow! Indeed, one of her most pronounced magical talents is bringing cooler temperatures to the mind and emotions. In the Victorian language of the flowers, her meaning is "do not abuse," which hints at her ability to assuage anger and violence. Similarly, crocus can help banish nightmares and generally infuse your dreamscapes with a cool serenity. For either purpose, bring a crocus or two into your bedroom, or place a couple of drops of the flower essence (a homeopathic remedy made from the blossom's vibration) under the tongue. Because crocus reminds us of vibrant beauty even in the most wintry landscape, she's also a harbinger and symbol of happiness. Saffron actually comes from the stigmas and styles of a variety of crocus, so to conjure happiness, spice your food with saffron or place a pinch into a charm bag along with a citrine quartz and nine allspice berries and carry it near your heart. Thanks to its rich color and precious value, saffron also possesses potent wealth energy, which you can access by incorporating saffron in abundance potions, rituals, charms, and baths.

—Tess Whitehurst

17 Saturday

4th ♐
☽ v/c 2:25 pm
Color: Indigo

18 Sunday

4th ♐
☽ enters ♑ 7:04 am
Color: Orange

Black pepper oil grants courage,
mental alertness, and physical energy

January

19 Monday

4th ♑
☽ v/c 5:51 am
Color: Silver

Birthday of Martin Luther King, Jr. (observed)

☽ Tuesday
4th ♑
☉ enters ♒ 4:43 am
☽ enters ♒ 7:59 am
New Moon 8:14 am
Color: Red

Sun enters Aquarius

21 Wednesday
1st ♒
☿ ℞ 10:54 am
☽ v/c 8:45 pm
Color: White

Celtic Tree Month of Rowan begins
Mercury retrorgrade until February 11

22 Thursday

1st ♒
☽ enters ♓ 7:48 am
Color: Turquoise

23 Friday

1st ♓
☽ v/c 6:13 am
Color: Pink

Use a rowan wand in healing spells

Set in Eastern Standard Time (EST)

Beet Cake

½ pound beets, roasted (about 4)
3 eggs
½ cup olive oil
½ cup honey
1 scant cup almond flour (you can grind almonds in coffee maker or food processor). You may substitute wheat, millet, or coconut flour.
½ cup unsweetened cocoa powder
1 tsp. baking powder
¼ tsp. baking soda
½ tsp. salt
½ tsp. cinnamon, nutmeg, vanilla, ginger (optional, to taste)

In earlier times, people relied on root vegetables such as potatoes, carrots, and beets to get through the winter. The roasted beets honor that hardship and are a beautiful, promising, Brigid-worthy red when roasted and skinned.

Preheat oven to 350 degrees F. In food processor or blender, puree beets, eggs, and olive oil. Add honey. Add remaining dry ingredients. Mix well. Pour into a greased cake pan or into a series of lined cupcake/muffin tin pans. Bake for 45 minutes, checking at the 30-minute mark with a toothpick. Done when toothpick comes out clean.

—Diana Rajchel

24 Saturday
1st ♓
☽ enters ♈ 8:31 am
Color: Gray

Gold represents masculinity, luxury, and projective energy

25 Sunday
1st ♈
Color: Amber

◐ Monday
1st ♈
☽ v/c 9:23 am
☽ enters ♉ 11:37 am
2nd quarter 11:48 pm
Color: Lavender

27 Tuesday
2nd ♉
♀ enters ♓ 10:00 am
☽ v/c 9:18 pm
Color: Black

*To hear secret thoughts, burn a blue candle
and concentrate on opening your mind*

28 Wednesday
2nd ♉
♇ enters ♒ 2:43 pm
☽ enters ♊ 5:36 pm
Color: Topaz

29 Thursday
2nd ♊
Color: White

Moldavite widens perspective and allows communication with the higher self

30 Friday
2nd ♊
☽ v/c 4:24 am
Color: Purple

Imbolc – Starting Clean and Clear

Imbolc originated as a Celtic fire festival that celebrated the first stirrings of spring. Its name is said to come from a word that means "in the belly," which may refer to the life beginning to sprout under the earth or to the baby lambs that are often born at this time. Magickally and practically, this is a good time for new beginnings and setting your goals for the year. Because Imbolc is also a time of cleansing and purification, consider

performing a simple ritual that combines both aspects of the holiday.

First, start with a ritual bath or shower. Use a sea salt scrub (easily made by combining sea salt and a few dried herbs like rosemary and peppermint) to gently scrub away old skin and old patterns. After bathing, smudge yourself with a sage stick. Now you can start your new journey.

Light a white candle and sit quietly with a pen and a pad or maybe your Book of Shadows. Write down your everyday (mundane) goals, then your spiritual and magickal ones. Be specific, be reasonable, but don't be afraid to set goals you'll have to work hard to attain. It's a new beginning, after all, and the sky's the limit.

—Deborah Blake

31 Saturday

2nd ♊
☽ enters ♋ 2:09 am
Color: Brown

1 Sunday

2nd ♋
☽ v/c 8:37 am
Color: Orange

*Arianhod is the Welsh
goddess of reincarnation,
called She of the Silver Wheel*

February

2 Monday

2nd ♋
☽ enters ♌ 12:41 pm
Color: Lavender

Imbolc
Groundhog Day

☺ Tuesday
2nd ♌
Full Moon 6:09 pm
Color: Gray

Quickening Moon

4 Wednesday

3rd ♌
☽ v/c 12:31 am
Color: White

Imbolc crossquarter day
(Sun reaches 15° Aquarius)

5 Thursday
3rd ♌
☽ enters ♍ 12:46 am
Color: Purple

6 Friday
3rd ♍
☽ v/c 5:09 pm
Color: Coral

Set in Eastern Standard Time (EST)

Magha Purnima (India)

Magha Purnima, the Full Moon day for this Hindu month, is a water festival. Hindus believe bathing in the Ganges on this day is a great purifying act (as is bathing in the sea or in any holy stream, river, or even a pool or pond). People walk for miles to partake in bathing festivals held at spots along the banks of the Yamuna, Sarayu, Narmad, and other holy rivers. A large tank that is considered holy at Kumbhkonam, near Madras, is a popular destination since Hindus believe that on this day, the Ganges flows into the tank. Libations are offered to dead ancestors, while donations of food, clothes, and money are given to the poor.

If you can't go to a river or the sea, take a ritual bath at home. Light candles in the bathroom, and incense if you like. Run a warm bath and add scented oils or herbs, preferably to match the incense. Play relaxing music or natural sounds if you can. Immerse yourself in the tub, and relax completely. Empty your mind of negative thoughts, and concentrate on the feel of the water, the scents, the sounds, the candlelight. When you are done, pull the plug and visualize all negative influences going down the drain.

—Magenta Griffith

---

7 Saturday
3rd ♍
☽ enters ♎ 1:44 pm
Color: Blue

Lily of the valley stands for sweetness and humility

---

8 Sunday
3rd ♎
Color: Amber

February

9 Monday

3rd ♎

☽ v/c 6:58 am

Color: Silver

10 Tuesday

3rd ♎

☽ enters ♏ 2:05 am

Color: Maroon

Cubeb berries help find a new lover

◐ Wednesday

3rd ♏

☿ D 9:57 am

4th quarter 10:50 pm

Color: Yellow

Yellow inspires vitality and change

12 Thursday

4th ♏

☽ v/c 12:32 am

☽ enters ♐ 11:46 am

Color: White

Gyan mudra: touch the tips of your thumb
and index finger for wisdom and enlightenment

13 Friday

4th ♐

Color: Rose

14 Saturday
4th ♐
☽ v/c 10:15 am
☽ enters ♑ 5:24 pm
Color: Brown

Valentine's Day

15 Sunday
4th ♑
Color: Gold

Violet leaf helps heal a broken heart

February

16 Monday
4th ♑
☽ v/c 3:17 pm
☽ enters ♒ 7:13 pm
Color: White

Presidents' Day (observed)

17 Tuesday
4th ♒
Color: Black

Mardi Gras (Fat Tuesday)

Wednesday
4th ♒
☽ v/c 6:47 pm
New Moon 6:47 pm
☽ enters ♓ 6:47 pm
☉ enters ♓ 6:50 pm
Color: Topaz

Ash Wednesday
Sun enters Pisces
Celtic Tree Month of Ash begins

19 Thursday
1st ♓
☽ v/c 6:02 pm
♂ enters ♈ 7:11 pm
Color: Green

Chinese New Year (sheep)

20 Friday
1st ♓
♀ enters ♈ 3:05 pm
☽ enters ♈ 6:13 pm
Color: Pink

Set in Eastern Standard Time (EST)

Camellia

One of camellia's many magical properties is the ability to help us attract and maintain friendships. You might write a magical intention related to friendship (in the present tense, as if it's already true, and avoiding naming a specific person) on a piece of paper and place it under a pink pillar candle on a dinner plate. Then arrange camellia blossoms around the outside and light. Camellia can also help boost your energy, especially by guiding you to activities for which you possess a natural affinity and passion. Similarly, she helps us acquire confidence by grounding us in our authenticity and reminding us of our inherent gifts. For either purpose, you might visit a blossoming camellia and sit in quiet contemplation with her, or take 2 to 3 drops of the flower essence (a homeopathic remedy) under the tongue once or twice per day. Because blessings flow to us most abundantly when we are in a relaxed, trusting state of receptivity, camellia helps us experience prosperity and luxury. As you can see, camellia's plentiful gifts center on helping us trust the process of life and feel comfortable in our own skin. Consequently, she's also excellent at helping us make decisions and trust our hunches.

—Tess Whitehurst

21 Saturday
1st ♈
☽ v/c 7:36 pm
Color: Gray

22 Sunday
1st ♈
☽ enters ♉ 7:28 pm
Color: Yellow

A staff of ash may command the waters

February/March

23 Monday
1st ♉
☽ v/c 9:57 pm
Color: Ivory

Ylang-ylang oil brings a sense of peace

24 Tuesday
1st ♉
☽ enters ♊ 11:54 pm
Color: Scarlet

Asteroid Pallas grants creative intelligence and mastery of talent

☽ Wednesday
1st ♊
2nd quarter 12:14 pm
Color: Brown

26 Thursday
2nd ♊
☽ v/c 3:43 am
Color: Crimson

27 Friday
2nd ♊
☽ enters ♋ 7:50 am
Color: Purple

Ananke is the Greek goddess of inevitability, compulsion, and necessity

Set in Eastern Standard Time (EST)

28 Saturday

2nd ♋
☽ v/c 12:53 pm
Color: Black

Nasturtium represents victory and conquest

1 Sunday

2nd ♋
☽ enters ♌ 6:34 pm
Color: Amber

2 Monday

2nd ♌
Color: White

Use an athame when working spells with the divine masculine

3 Tuesday

2nd ♌
☽ v/c 3:48 am
Color: Gray

Black provides safety, banishing, and binding

4 Wednesday

2nd ♌
☽ enters ♍ 6:58 am
Color: Topaz

☺ Thursday

2nd ♍
Full Moon 1:05 pm
☽ v/c 1:36 pm
Color: Crimson

Purim
Storm Moon

6 Friday

3rd ♍
☽ enters ♎ 7:52 pm
Color: Pink

Spring Lantern Festival (China)

Spring Lantern Festival is the last day of the traditional Chinese New Year's celebrations. It's a holiday for appreciating the bright Full Moon and for family gatherings. People watch the Lion Dance and stilt-walking performances. During the Lantern Festival, children go out at night to temples carrying red paper lanterns and solve riddles written on the lanterns. Because appreciating the lanterns offers a good chance for boys and girls to mingle, the Lantern Festival may be regarded as the Chinese equivalent of Valentine's Day. It is also known as the Yuanxiao Festival because everyone eats yuanxiao, a round rice ball whose shape suggests the Full Moon. It is stuffed with fillings such as sugar, rose petals, sesame, sweetened bean paste, or jujube paste. Yuanxiao can be boiled, fried, or steamed.

Do you have any riddles you are fond of? Host a Full Moon viewing for your friends and have everyone bring their favorite riddle written on a slip of paper. Draw them out of a Chinese lantern, if you can find one, or out of a hat, and see who knows the answers. Serve round Chinese dumplings if available, or plain round balls of sweetened white rice.

—Magenta Griffith

7 Saturday
3rd ♎
Color: Blue

8 Sunday
3rd ♎
☽ v/c 9:24 pm
Color: Gold

Daylight Saving Time begins at 2 am

March

9 Monday

3rd ♎︎
☽ enters ♏︎ 9:10 am
Color: Lavender

10 Tuesday

3rd ♏︎
Color: White

Bury an object in salt to remove negative influences

11 Wednesday

3rd ♏︎
☽ v/c 3:46 pm
☽ enters ♐︎ 7:30 pm
Color: Brown

12 Thursday

3rd ♐︎
☿ enters ♓︎ 11:52 pm
Color: Purple

Pray to Ama-Tsu-Mara,
the Shinto god of smiths,
for skill in craftsmanship

◯ Friday

3rd ♐︎
4th quarter 1:48 pm
✳ D 3:42 pm
☽ v/c 7:11 pm
Color: Coral

Set in Eastern Daylight Time (EDT)

Deviled Eggs

Eggs symbolize rebirth in Pagan and Christian traditions. They also pose the same question each spring to these families: "Now what do we do with all these boiled eggs?"

6 whole eggs
½ cup mayonnaise
1 T. lemon juice
½ cup mustard, or
   2 tsp. mustard powder
⅛ cup pickle juice
Paprika or chili powder

Hard-boil the eggs. After cooling, remove from shells, running under water to wash off any excess. Slice each egg lengthwise down the middle. Remove the yolks from the centers, being careful not to damage the egg whites. Set the egg whites on a plate and put the yolks in a mixing bowl. In the bowl, add the mayonnaise, lemon juice, mustard, pickle juice, and paprika or chili powder to taste. Mash with a fork until the mixture has a fluffy texture. With a spoon, fill each of the egg whites with the yolk mixture. Garnish with paprika or chili powder as desired.

—Diana Rajchel

14 Saturday

4th ♐
☽ enters ♑ 2:40 am
♄ Rℵ 11:02 am
Color: Black

15 Sunday

4th ♑
Color: Orange

Hakini mudra: spread hands and touch tips of all fingers and thumbs together to aid concentration

March

16 Monday

4th ♑
☽ v/c 4:02 am
☽ enters ♒ 6:14 am
Color: Gray

Use hyssop oil for purification

17 Tuesday

4th ♒
♀ enters ♉ 6:15 am
☽ v/c 2:18 pm
Color: Maroon

St. Patrick's Day

18 Wednesday

4th ♒
☽ enters ♓ 6:58 am
Color: Yellow

Celtic Tree Month of Alder begins

19 Thursday

4th ♓
Color: Turquoise

☽ Friday

4th ♓
☽ v/c 5:36 am
New Moon 5:36 am
☽ enters ♈ 6:28 am
☉ enters ♈ 6:45 pm
Color: White

Ostara/Spring Equinox
Sun enters Aries
International Astrology Day
Solar eclipse 5:45 am, 29° ♓ 29'

Ostara – Eostre Eggs

For those who live in the colder climates, spring usually comes as a huge relief after the winter's chill and darkness. The light returns, buds appear on the trees, flowers begin to blossom, and nature celebrates with myriad forms of new life. Birds sit on nests full of eggs and tiny baby bunnies nibble at the first green grasses. Is it any wonder that our celebration of Ostara is symbolized by eggs, chicks, rabbits, and early blooming plants like crocus and tulips?

Ostara is all about fertility, youth, and new growth. This is the time of the goddess as Maiden; young, joyous, and full of life. She invites us to join in the celebration, so why not use this time to return to your own youth and do something fun and meaningful? Many folks grew up decorating Easter eggs, but now know we can call them Eostre eggs, after the vernal goddess.

You can do this by yourself or with your family or friends. Decorate some hard-boiled eggs with Pagan symbols that suit the season, like runes for new beginnings (Beorc), pentacles, flowers, or animals. Place them on your altar with some fresh flowers and celebrate spring and your own new beginnings.

—Deborah Blake

---

21 Saturday
1st ♈
☽ v/c 6:51 pm
Color: Indigo

A whistle of alder wood may summon and control the winds

---

22 Sunday
1st ♈
☽ enters ♉ 6:40 am
Color: Yellow

March

23 Monday
1st ♉
☽ v/c 10:25 am
Color: Silver

24 Tuesday
1st ♉
☽ enters ♊ 9:23 am
Color: Black

*Tie knots in a cord to capture the wind;
then untie them to release it when needed*

25 Wednesday
1st ♊
Color: White

*Asteroid Cruithne traces a path of personal
transformation and connection with the earth*

26 Thursday
1st ♊
☽ v/c 8:35 am
☽ enters ♋ 3:45 pm
Color: Green

☽ Friday
1st ♋
2nd quarter 3:43 am
Color: Rose

Set in Eastern Daylight Time (EDT)

Cherry Blossom

Ahh, the vibrant candy-pinkness of a cherry blossom! Beloved in Japan, cherry blossoms are earthly manifestations of divine love and can help align us very powerfully with God/Goddess/All That Is. As such, cherry blossoms are great for clearing energy and raising vibrations. For example, you might use a small bouquet or branch to sweep your aura or to sweep the energy of a room. (Just sweep the surrounding air.) You can also place a few drops of cherry blossom essence in a mister of rose water and use it as a room- or aura-clearing spray. If forgiveness (of yourself or someone else) is one of your magical goals, spending quality time with a blossoming cherry tree or taking a few drops of flower essence under the tongue can help you let go and heal. Cherry blossoms in your home or bathwater can help soothe harshness and stress and bring gentleness and softness to the spirit. This flower is also renowned as a love charm. Author Scott Cunningham says that to draw love, you might "tie a single strand of your hair to a blossoming cherry tree." Similarly, you might hold a few cherry blossoms to your heart and affirm that you are ready to open your heart to love.

—Tess Whitehurst

28 Saturday

2nd ♋
⚸ enters ♓ 1:53 pm
☽ v/c 9:58 pm
Color: Brown

Carry abrus seeds in an amulet pouch for good luck

29 Sunday

2nd ♋
☽ enters ♌ 1:48 am
Color: Gold

Palm Sunday

30 Monday
2nd ♌
☽ v/c 9:57 am
☿ enters ♈ 9:44 pm
Color: White

Haumi is the Maori god of wild food, helpful to gatherers

31 Tuesday
2nd ♌
♂ enters ♉ 12:26 pm
☽ enters ♍ 2:12 pm
Color: Red

1 Wednesday
2nd ♍
Color: Yellow

April Fools' Day (All Fools' Day—Pagan)

2 Thursday
2nd ♍
☽ v/c 5:01 am
Color: White

3 Friday
2nd ♍
☽ enters ♎ 3:07 am
♀ enters ♒ 8:21 am
Color: Rose

Good Friday

Hanuman Jayanti (India)

In India, Hanuman Jayanti is celebrated as the birthday of Lord
Hanuman, the monkey-headed god.
The monkey-God Hanuman is widely
venerated throughout India, and
his temples can be found the entire
length and breadth of the country.
Hanuman is the representation of
strength and energy and is said to be
able to assume any form at will. He
can move mountains, dart through
the air, seize the clouds and rival

Garuda (a mythical giant bird) in swiftness of flight. He is worshiped in
folk tradition as a deity with magical powers and the ability to conquer
evil spirits and other powerful negative energies. He is depicted with a
ruby-red face, yellow skin, a shining gold coat, and an immensely long
tail. Sindhur, a red powder made from vermillion, is applied to the body of
the Hanuman statues and offerings are made of appalu, a sweet rice-flour
pancake that is deep-fried in oil. His great adventures are related in great
detail in the Ramayana, one of the two epics of Hinduism.

On this day, fairs are organized at some of the temples, so this might
be an auspicious day to organize a fair, especially a fund-raiser for charity.

—Magenta Griffith

☻ Saturday

2nd ♎
Full Moon 8:06 am
☽ v/c 11:59 am
Color: Brown

Wind Moon
Passover begins
Lunar eclipse 8:00 am, 14° ♎ 21'

---

5 Sunday

3rd ♎
☽ enters ♏ 3:04 pm
Color: Yellow

Easter

---

6 Monday
3rd ♏
Color: Gray

Ginseng root enhances male virility

7 Tuesday
3rd ♏
☽ v/c 4:42 pm
Color: White

Lay a broom across the doorway
for protection against malicious forces

8 Wednesday
3rd ♏
☽ enters ♐ 1:08 am
♃ D 12:57 pm
☿ enters ♑ 10:48 pm
Color: Brown

9 Thursday
3rd ♐
☽ v/c 1:42 pm
Color: Purple

10 Friday
3rd ♐
☽ enters ♑ 8:47 am
Color: Pink

Orthodox Good Friday

○ **Saturday**

3rd ♑

♀ enters ♊ 11:28 am

4th quarter 11:44 pm

Color: Black

Passover ends

12 **Sunday**

4th ♑

☽ v/c 4:15 am

☽ enters ♒ 1:44 pm

Color: Amber

Orthodox Easter

April

13 Monday
4th ≈
Color: Silver

Wear zoisite jewelry to boost your enthusiasm

14 Tuesday
4th ≈
☽ v/c 3:45 pm
☽ enters ♓ 4:12 pm
☿ enters ♉ 6:51 pm
Color: Maroon

15 Wednesday
4th ♓
☽ v/c 5:37 pm
Color: Topaz

Celtic Tree Month of Willow begins

16 Thursday
4th ♓
☽ enters ♈ 5:00 pm
♇ ℞ 11:56 pm
Color: White

17 Friday
4th ♈
Color: Coral

Prana mudra: touch the tips of your little finger,
ring finger, and thumb together while extending
the middle and index fingers to increase vitality

Rhubarb Almond Crumble

Rhubarb is one of the first plants to thrive in spring. Its appearance heralds the end of the frost and the beginning of the warm season.

4 stems rhubarb
1 cup ground almonds
2 T. liquid stevia or stevia leaf
  (do NOT use the type served
  with drinks)
½ cup honey or molasses, if desired

To save time, preheat the oven to 375 degrees F while preparing the other ingredients, which can include grinding the almonds if you choose. To prepare, boil the rhubarb until tender. Add a shot or two of stevia glycerin to the water to sweeten. The result will still be tart, but milder than the taste of the plant all by itself. Reserve the juice for a beverage.

Put the rhubarb in a baking dish and pour in the ground almonds. Stir. Add honey or molasses if desired. Bake for 10 minutes.

—Diana Rajchel

☽ Saturday

4th ♈
☽ v/c 2:57 pm
New Moon 2:57 pm
☽ enters ♉ 5:31 pm
Color: Blue

Include willow wood in a charm to grant wishes

---

19 Sunday

1st ♉
☽ v/c 7:07 pm
♀ ℞ 9:29 pm
Color: Orange

April

20 Monday

1st ♉
☉ enters ♉ 5:42 am
☽ enters ♊ 7:28 pm
Color: Ivory

Sun enters Taurus

21 Tuesday

1st ♊
Color: Gray

Mixed zinnias represent memories of absent friends

22 Wednesday

1st ♊
☽ v/c 1:38 am
Color: Yellow

Earth Day; the first Earth Day was in 1970

23 Thursday

1st ♊
☽ enters ♋ 12:25 am
Color: Crimson

24 Friday

1st ♋
☽ v/c 1:04 pm
Color: White

Uzume is the Shinto goddess of joy and happiness

Beltane – Love in Abundance

Beltane falls on the first day of May. Some folks celebrate on May Eve with a bonfire, which is fitting since Beltane is a fire festival derived from a word for "bright fire." Others observe the holiday at noon, with the springtime sun serving as the fire.

Beltane can be a boisterous and bawdy holiday, since it focuses on abundance, fertility, and love. The God and Goddess, who are at the height of their power and vigor, join together in passion to bring life back to the earth. Pagans often celebrate with feasting, a dance around the Maypole, and all acts sensual and sexual.

But Beltane isn't just about lust and romance—it also celebrates abundance, growth, and increase. If you need to bring more of anything into your life—money, love, health—this is a good time to do that type of magickal work. It is also a good time to show your love for your significant other, family, friends, pets, or even our Mother, the Earth.

Instead of a Maypole, try using a May bush. (Plant a new one or use an existing bush or potted plant.) Tie ribbons on it to symbolize the things you wish to increase in your life and dance with joy, your heart filled with love.

—Deborah Blake

○ **Saturday**
1st ♋
☽ enters ♌ 9:13 am
2nd quarter 7:55 pm
Color: Indigo

26 Sunday
2nd ♌
Color: Amber

Throwing grain at newlyweds
will encourage fertility and abundance

27 Monday
2nd ♌
☽ v/c 10:12 am
☽ enters ♍ 9:07 pm
Color: Lavender

Peppermint oil strengthens the conscious mind

28 Tuesday
2nd ♍
Color: Red

29 Wednesday
2nd ♍
Color: White

Asteroid Lilith foments rebellion, but also freedom and justice

30 Thursday
2nd ♍
☽ v/c 8:23 am
☽ enters ♎ 10:03 am
♀ enters ♐ 1:59 pm
☿ enters ♊ 10:00 pm
Color: Turquoise

1 Friday
2nd ♎
Color: Coral

Beltane/May Day

Vesak (Buddhist)

Buddha Purnima, or Vesak, is a holiday celebrating the birthday of the Buddha. The Full Moon in May commemorates his birth, enlightenment, and death. Devout Buddhists are expected to assemble in their temples before dawn. Hymns are sung in praise of the holy triple gem: the Buddha, the Dharma (his teachings), and the Sangha (his disciples). Devotees may bring simple offerings of flowers, candles, and incense to lay at the feet of their teacher. These symbolic offerings are to remind followers that just as the beautiful flowers wither away after a short while, and the candles and incense soon burn out, so too is life subject to decay and destruction. Devotees are enjoined to make a special effort to refrain from killing of any kind, and are encouraged to partake of vegetarian food for the day.

This might be a good day to find out more about the teachings of the Buddha. Here are a few books you might read: *How To Practice: The Way to a Meaningful Life* by the Dalai Lama. *Buddhism: A Very Short Introduction* by Damien Keown, *Buddhism: A Concise Introduction* by Huston Smith and Philip Novak, and *Buddhism Plain and Simple* by Steve Hagen.

—Magenta Griffith

---

2 Saturday
2nd ♎
☽ v/c 10:03 am
☽ enters ♏ 9:47 pm
Color: Indigo

Wear copper for fertility and passion

☺ Sunday
2nd ♏
Full Moon 11:42 pm
Color: Gold

Flower Moon

May

4 Monday
3rd ♏
☽ v/c 9:49 pm
Color: Ivory

5 Tuesday
3rd ♏
☽ enters ♐ 7:13 am
Color: Black

Cinco de Mayo
Beltane crossquarter day
(Sun reaches 15° Taurus)

6 Wednesday
3rd ♐
Color: Brown

7 Thursday
3rd ♐
☽ v/c 1:51 pm
☽ enters ♑ 2:16 pm
♀ enters ♋ 6:52 pm
Color: Crimson

Unakite on the altar attracts animal guides

8 Friday
3rd ♑
Color: White

Tulip

In Holland in the 1600s, the beauty of tulips caused a craze: the bulbs became so highly valued that they temporarily underscored the economy like gold. Indeed, this flower's most potent magical quality has to do with beauty: physical beauty, emotional beauty, and the beauty of life itself. For example, to increase the sensory appreciation of a meal or gathering, employ tulips as a centerpiece. Or, to shroud yourself in a veil of magnetism and desirability, try sweeping your aura with a few stems. Because of her substantial bulb and alignment with the senses and the physical world, tulip can also help us with grounding. So if you're feeling anxious, plant tulips, spend time with tulips, or take a few drops of the flower essence under your tongue. Tulip resonates at the heart, so if your heart—physical or emotional—could use some strengthening, try adding a few drops of the flower essence to your drinking water or bath. Tulip also shares a lot of qualities with love goddesses: earthiness, beauty, sensuality, heart-centeredness, and desirability. As such, she can be a great addition to love-goddess altars or rituals that involve goddesses such as Hathor, Aphrodite, Venus, or Parvati.

—Tess Whitehurst

9 Saturday

3rd ♑
☽ v/c 4:35 pm
☽ enters ♒ 7:22 pm
Color: Gray

Birrahgnooloo is an Australian fertility goddess who,
if properly asked, will send floods to replenish the fields

10 Sunday

3rd ♒
Color: Yellow

Mother's Day
Census Day (Canada)

May

◑ Monday

3rd ≈
☽ v/c 6:36 am
4th quarter 6:36 am
♂ enters ♊ 10:40 pm
☽ enters ♓ 10:53 pm
Color: Silver

*Silver represents femininity,
communication, and receptive energy*

12 Tuesday

4th ♓
Color: White

13 Wednesday

4th ♓
☽ v/c 12:55 pm
Color: Topaz

Celtic Tree Month of Hawthorn begins

14 Thursday

4th ♓
☽ enters ♈ 1:13 am
Color: Turquoise

15 Friday

4th ♈
☽ v/c 8:04 am
Color: Purple

Carry a piece of snakeskin in your wallet to attract wealth

Set in Eastern Daylight Time (EDT)

16 Saturday

4th ♈

☽ enters ♉ 3:02 am

Color: Black

*The Hindu god Kurma relates
to the virtue of perseverance,
and his symbol is the turtle*

17 Sunday

4th ♉

Color: Orange

May

☽ Monday

4th ♉
☽ v/c 12:13 am
New Moon 12:13 am
☽ enters ♊ 5:27 am
☿ ℞ 9:49 pm
Color: Lavender

Mercury retrograde until June 11

19 Tuesday

1st ♊
☽ v/c 1:57 pm
Color: Maroon

Asteroid Thereus brings the patience
of a hunter to the astrological chart

20 Wednesday

1st ♊
☽ enters ♋ 9:56 am
Color: White

Oleander blossoms urge caution

21 Thursday

1st ♋
☉ enters ♊ 4:45 am
☽ v/c 8:36 pm
Color: Purple

Sun enters Gemini

22 Friday

1st ♋
☽ enters ♌ 5:42 pm
Color: Coral

Set in Eastern Daylight Time (EDT)

Honeysuckle

Honeysuckle's energetic signature has to do with activating, unsticking, and getting things moving. This includes releasing things that no longer serve to enhance our life flow. Also, her heady, sensual scent can help us get out of our minds and into our bodies and to release fears and limiting beliefs about our sexuality. For this purpose, try simply inhaling the scent and spending time in quiet contemplation with a blossoming plant. You might also place a muslin charm bag with fresh blossoms near your bed. To get your finances flowing, dry seven blossoms and place them in a green charm bag with a silver dollar and a white quartz. Anoint with neroli or rose oil and keep in your purse or wallet. To release blocks to intuition, charge water in the light of the Full Moon and then use a honeysuckle blossom to anoint your belly, heart, and third eye with the water. Or place the charged water in a mister and add nine drops of honeysuckle essence. Then mist yourself or your space before doing divinatory work. Honeysuckle's magic can also help you let go of old circumstances to make room for new ones (e.g., when you move or begin a new job) and activating good luck.

—Tess Whitehurst

23 Saturday
1st ♌
Color: Blue

Tangerine oil strengthens a blend

24 Sunday
1st ♌
☽ v/c 6:50 am
Color: Amber

Shavuot

May

○ Monday
1st ♌
☽ enters ♍ 4:52 am
2nd quarter 1:19 pm
Color: White

Memorial Day (observed)

26 Tuesday
2nd ♍
☽ v/c 10:21 pm
Color: Gray

27 Wednesday
2nd ♍
☽ enters ♎ 5:42 pm
Color: Yellow

Bhudi mudra: touch the tips of the
thumb and little finger to deepen intuition

28 Thursday
2nd ♎
Color: Green

29 Friday
2nd ♎
☽ v/c 4:20 pm
Color: Pink

Azalea flowers say "Take care of yourself for me"

Set in Eastern Daylight Time (EDT)

30 Saturday

2nd ♎︎

☽ enters ♏︎ 5:34 am

Color: Brown

Ask the Norse goddess Gefjun for assistance with plowing and planting

31 Sunday

2nd ♏︎

Color: Yellow

June

1 Monday

2nd ♏︎
☽ v/c 7:01 am
☽ enters ♐︎ 2:39 pm
Color: Silver

Ask the Norse god Bragi for talent in poetry and music

☺ Tuesday
2nd ♐︎
Full Moon 12:19 pm
Color: Scarlet

Strong Sun Moon

3 Wednesday

3rd ♐︎
☿ ℞ 12:20 am
☽ v/c 1:59 am
☽ enters ♑︎ 8:50 pm
Color: White

4 Thursday

3rd ♑︎
Color: Purple

*Surround your bed with black stones to protect
against negative people and psychic vampires*

5 Friday

3rd ♑︎
☽ v/c 6:54 am
♀ enters ♌︎ 11:33 am
Color: Rose

Set in Eastern Daylight Time (EDT)

Vat Purnima (India)

In India, this Full Moon is Vat Purnima. It is primarily a woman's holiday, dedicated to the goddess Savitri. She saved her husband from a premature death by convincing the god of death, Yama, to spare him because of her purity and devotion. In imitation of Savitri, women fast all night. After breaking their fast, they bathe together, dress in traditional clothes and jewelry, and then gather fruits, clothes, and other items to give to charity. In some places, women worship a banyan tree, and water the tree; sometimes, they sprinkle red vermillion powder on it. Another practice, called parikrama, is to wrap cotton threads around the trees' trunks, going around it seven times. Later in the day, they visit the temples and offer prayers to the goddess Savitri and listen to her story. Traditional food also plays an important role in the Vat Purnima festival, because people visit each other and feast. Young people pay their respects to the elders. People wear new clothes and decorate their houses with colorful flowers.

For the full story of Savitri, check out "The Book of the Forest" section of the *Mahabharata*, one of the two major epic works of Hinduism.

—Magenta Griffith

---

6 Saturday

3rd ♑
☽ enters ♒ 1:02 am
⚷ enters ♈ 5:05 pm
Color: Gray

---

7 Sunday

3rd ♒
☽ v/c 10:30 am
Color: Amber

Green brings plant magic and personal growth

June

8 Monday

3rd ♒
☽ enters ♓ 4:16 am
Color: Lavender

Shuni mudra: touch the tips of thumb and middle finger for patience

○ Tuesday

3rd ♓
4th quarter 11:42 am
☽ v/c 2:08 pm
Color: White

10 Wednesday

4th ♓
☽ enters ♈ 7:14 am
Color: Brown

Celtic Tree Month of Oak begins

11 Thursday

4th ♈
☿ D 6:33 pm
☽ v/c 7:43 pm
Color: White

Use oak to fuel a midsummer or need fire

12 Friday

4th ♈
♆ ℞ 5:09 am
☽ enters ♉ 10:16 am
Color: Pink

Cold Avocado Soup

The heart of summer is a rich, beautiful time where fruit first starts to bear. Avocado, considered both fruit and nut—thus signifying the combined presence of God and Goddess—is a rich way to celebrate the beginning of the abundant season.

1 skinned and pitted avocado
1 T. lime juice
1 pinch salt
1 clove garlic
1 cup yogurt
Salsa (optional)
Cheese (optional)
Sour cream (optional)

Combine avocado, lime juice, salt, garlic, and yogurt in food processor or blender. Blend until smooth. Pour out into bowls. Garnish, if desired, with salsa, cheese, or sour cream. Serve immediately. This dish, paired with tomatoes, peppers, early summer fruits, lemonade or iced tea, and chips, is an excellent alternative to barbecued meats usually served around a Litha fire.

—Diana Rajchel

13 Saturday

4th ♉
☽ v/c 6:06 pm
Color: Black

Asteroid Iris reveals lies and rewards honesty

14 Sunday

4th ♉
☽ enters ♊ 1:51 pm
♄ enters ♏ 8:36 pm
Color: Gold

Flag Day

June

15 Monday

4th ♊
Color: Gray

Rain on a wedding means no tears in a marriage

☽ Tuesday

4th ♊
☽ v/c 10:05 am
New Moon 10:05 am
☽ enters ♋ 6:51 pm
Color: Red

Erebos is the Greek god of shadows and darkness

17 Wednesday

1st ♋
Color: Topaz

18 Thursday

1st ♋
Color: Crimson

Ramadan begins

19 Friday

1st ♋
☽ v/c 1:52 am
☽ enters ♌ 2:23 am
Color: White

Set in Eastern Daylight Time (EDT)

Summer Solstice – Fire and Light

The Summer Solstice is the longest day of the year, and the shortest night. This is when summer has truly arrived, full of light, warmth, and abundance. The Goddess is pregnant with the child of her consort, the Sun god, and so we celebrate life, motherhood, and the love of family.

Midsummer is a customary time for handfastings, as well as the perfect time for celebrations that include children and family. It is traditional to throw lavender on the bonfire as a sacrifice to the old gods, and some believe that this is the optimal day to harvest your magickal herbs. Litha marks the end of the waxing time of year and the rule of the Oak King, and begins the waning half, ruled by the Holly King.

The Summer Solstice is all about abundance and celebration of the light, so why not have a big feast for friends and family to celebrate with you? Cook over the bonfire or barbeque, but remember to include traditional summer dishes and local seasonal foods. Strawberries dipped in chocolate or beautiful, ripe peaches dripping with juice are a perfect symbol of summer's vibrant energy. Then stay up late to enjoy the longest day of the year!

—Deborah Blake

20 Saturday

1st ♌
Color: Blue

It is good luck to see a spider spinning a web in the morning

21 Sunday

1st ♌
☽ v/c 12:09 pm
☉ enters ♋ 12:38 pm
☽ enters ♍ 12:59 pm
Color: Yellow

Father's Day
Sun enters Cancer
Midsummer/Litha/Summer Solstice

June

22 Monday
1st ♍
Color: White

To attract an item to you, draw a symbol of it
on a leaf with a burnt stick, and pin the leaf to a tree

23 Tuesday
1st ♍
Color: Black

Viscaria blossoms ask for a dance

◖ Wednesday
1st ♍
☽ v/c 1:12 am
☽ enters ♎ 1:41 am
2nd quarter 7:03 am
☿ ℞ 7:36 am
♂ enters ♋ 9:33 am
Color: Yellow

25 Thursday
2nd ♎
☽ v/c 7:22 pm
Color: Green

Use vetiver oil to protect your finances

26 Friday
2nd ♎
☽ enters ♏ 1:57 pm
Color: Purple

Set in Eastern Daylight Time (EDT)

27 Saturday

2nd ♏

Color: Brown

28 Sunday

2nd ♏

☽ v/c 9:50 pm
☽ enters ♐ 11:21 pm
Color: Orange

Pyrite cubes on a desk enhance logic, memory, and clarity

June/July

29 Monday
2nd ♐
Color: Lavender

Reshef, the Syrian god of war and thunder,
can send or withhold dangerous storms

30 Tuesday
2nd ♐
☽ v/c 2:18 pm
☿ enters ♍ 6:59 pm
Color: Gray

☺ Wednesday
2nd ♐
☽ enters ♑ 5:11 am
Full Moon 10:20 pm
Color: Topaz

Blessing Moon

2 Thursday
3rd ♑
Color: White

3 Friday
3rd ♑
☽ v/c 6:38 am
☽ enters ♒ 8:21 am
Color: Pink

White features purity, innocence, and cleansing;
in candle or stone magic, it can substitute for any other color

Set in Eastern Daylight Time (EDT)

Guru Purnima (India)

This Full Moon is Guru Purnima, a festival traditionally celebrated in India. The word guru is derived from two Sanskrit words, *Gu* means "ignorance," *Ru* means "the remover of ignorance"; thus, the one who removes our ignorance is a guru. On this day, followers pay their regards to their guru or spiritual guide, who many believe is a necessary part of their lives. The festival is common to all traditions in Hinduism because it is dedicated to respect for their religious teachers and leaders. Hindus also celebrate it in honor of the great sage Vyasa, who is seen as one of the greatest gurus in ancient Hindu traditions, and floral offerings and symbolic gifts are given away in his name. Vyasa was not only believed to have been born on this day, but also to have started writing the *Brahma Sutras*, a major religious text at this time. Recitations of these sutras, dedicated to him, are organized on this day.

This would be a good day to write a letter to someone who has helped you on your spiritual path, whether or not you call them a guru. If they are no longer alive, write the letter and burn it while thinking about them.

—Magenta Griffith

4 Saturday

3rd ≈
Color: Black

Independence Day

5 Sunday

3rd ≈
☽ v/c 8:32 am
☽ enters ♓ 10:23 am
Color: Yellow

July

6 Monday

3rd ♓
Color: Lavender

7 Tuesday

3rd ♓
☽ v/c 10:36 am
☽ enters ♈ 12:38 pm
Color: Red

Use red for assertiveness and competition

☽ Wednesday

3rd ♈
☿ enters ♋ 2:52 pm
4th quarter 4:24 pm
Color: Brown

Celtic Tree Month of Holly begins

9 Thursday

4th ♈
☽ v/c 9:47 am
☽ enters ♉ 3:49 pm
Color: Green

10 Friday

4th ♉
Color: Purple

Kubera mudra:
touch tips of thumb and first two fingers,
curling other fingers to palm, for achieving goals

Set in Eastern Daylight Time (EDT)

Peony

Luxurious, lush, delicious-smelling peony was named after a Greek student of Asclepius with healing abilities so enviable that Zeus had to rescue him from his teacher's jealous rage by transforming him into a flower. With that in mind, ancient Greek medicine featured peony prominently as a versatile and potent healing plant. Energetically and magically, peonies can facilitate healing by simply keeping a fresh bouquet nearby (or in the form of a flower essence). Peony also lends himself powerfully to healing rituals and spells. In China, the peony is associated with wealth and honor, and in Japan, growing peony was a sign of prosperity. Indeed, peony exudes a feeling of affluent splendor. He is also relaxing, being used historically as an antispasmodic and sedative. Today, his vibration can be extremely useful when preparing for job interviews or presentations, simply by spending time in quiet contemplation with a peony and requesting assistance, imbibing the flower essence, or incorporating the blossoms, petals, or seeds into charms created to calm confidence and relieve anxiety. Additionally, peony has been used in magic related to cleansing, shielding, and protecting.

—Tess Whitehurst

---

11 Saturday

4th ♉
☽ v/c 5:52 pm
☽ enters ♊ 8:16 pm
Color: Indigo

Holly leaves or crown grant purification and consecration

---

12 Sunday

4th ♊
Color: Amber

Orange is the color of vitality, fun, and self-expression

July

13 Monday
4th ♊
☽ v/c 11:31 pm
Color: Gray

14 Tuesday
4th ♊
☽ enters ♋ 2:14 am
Color: White

*Seneca snake root protects against
liars, backstabbers, and false friends*

☽ Wednesday
4th ♋
New Moon 9:24 pm
Color: Yellow

Rub a piece of calcite for aid in solving problems

16 Thursday
1st ♋
☽ v/c 7:24 am
☽ enters ♌ 10:15 am
Color: Purple

17 Friday
1st ♌
Color: Rose

Ramadan ends

Set in Eastern Daylight Time (EDT)

Baked Kohlrabi

Grain is far from the only harvest to begin at Lughnasadh. Kohlrabi, a spicy root vegetable common in the Midwest, reminds us that the God is about to go to ground.

2 large kohlrabies
2 T. olive or sunflower oil
1 tsp. sea salt
1 tsp. garlic powder
1 tsp. paprika
1 tsp. chili powder
1 tsp. coriander

Preheat oven to 350 degrees F. Peel the outer layer of kohlrabi. Slice the center into strips. In a bowl, mix the oil and spices. Add the kohlrabi and stir thoroughly, getting each piece layered in the oil. Spread out evenly on a cookie sheet. Bake for 10 to 15 minutes. Serve hot.

Kohlrabi is a common part of the first harvest in the United States, which makes it a perfect Lughnasadh dish. It also goes well with most any food from the garden this time of year, including breads, berries, and other fruit from the land.

—Diana Rajchel

18 Saturday
1st ♌
☽ v/c 5:41 pm
♀ enters ♍ 6:38 pm
☽ enters ♍ 8:47 pm
Color: Blue

19 Sunday
1st ♍
Color: Orange

Ahamkara mudra: touch the tip of thumb to outside
of first finger at the middle knuckle to boost confidence

July

20 Monday
1st ♍
Color: White

Yellow tulips mean "There's sunshine in your smile"

21 Tuesday
1st ♍
☽ v/c 6:07 am
☽ enters ♎ 9:23 am
Color: Maroon

Labradorite in the bedroom relieves stress and brings gentle sleep

22 Wednesday
1st ♎
☉ enters ♌ 11:30 pm
Color: White

Sun enters Leo

23 Thursday
1st ♎
☿ enters ♌ 8:14 am
☽ v/c 2:12 pm
☽ enters ♏ 10:07 pm
Color: Crimson

○ Friday
1st ♏
2nd quarter 12:04 am
Color: Coral

Pink promotes domestic harmony,
protection of children,
spiritual and emotional healing

Set in Eastern Daylight Time (EDT)

Lammas – Breaking Bread

Lammas is the first of three harvest festivals. Most specifically, it celebrates the grain harvest, which so many early cultures depended on to get them (and their animals) through the winter. The wheat stands high in the fields, and corn is ripe or ripening. Harvest festivals are a time for rejoicing, but also a time to appreciate the food on our tables, which so many have worked hard to produce.

These days, we tend to be quite distant from the people who grow our food; often the fruits or vegetables come from other countries or are shipped across country. Migrant workers work long, hard hours in backbreaking conditions to grow the food we buy in a grocery store. Take a moment, on this day which celebrates the harvest, to think about where your food comes from, and give thanks to those who grow and harvest it. And if you can, support your local farmers.

All cultures have some form of "breaking bread together" tradition—cooking and eating together almost always brings people closer. So why not bake your own bread and share it with your friends? You can use a mix, but get your hands in there and knead it. Then spread with butter and enjoy!

—Deborah Blake

---

25 Saturday

2nd ♏
♀ ℞ 5:29 am
Color: Black

Venus retrograde until September 6

---

26 Sunday

2nd ♏
☽ v/c 5:14 am
♅ ℞ 6:38 am
☽ enters ♐ 8:24 am
Color: Gold

It's unlucky to wear a garment while mending it

July/August

27 Monday
2nd ♐
Color: Silver

Ningirsu is the Sumerian god of rain, irrigation, and fertility

28 Tuesday
2nd ♐
☽ v/c 9:36 am
☽ enters ♑ 2:47 pm
Color: Black

29 Wednesday
2nd ♑
Color: Brown

*Tou-Mou, the Chinese goddess
of the pole star, keeps
the records of the Immortals*

30 Thursday
2nd ♑
☽ v/c 2:50 pm
☽ enters ♒ 5:40 pm
Color: Turquoise

Wormwood oil breaks spells

☺ Friday
2nd ♒
Full Moon 6:43 am
♀ enters ♌ 11:27 am
Color: White

Blue Moon

Set in Eastern Daylight Time (EDT)

Blue Moon

Today is a Blue Moon, in most people's opinion, but there are three different definitions of a Blue Moon. The most common usage today is the second Full Moon in a single calendar month, which happens every two or three years. Use of the term "blue moon" in that way comes from a misinterpretation of the traditional definition that appeared in the March 1946 issue of the magazine *Sky and Telescope*. Prior to that time, the term was used to describe the third Full Moon in a season with four, a season being defined as the time period between a solstice and an equinox, or vice versa. The third definition of a Blue Moon is two Full Moons in the same astrological sign. Because a blue moon is uncommon, the term "once in a blue moon" is used to mean a rare event. The term has nothing to do with the actual color of the moon.

The next Blue Moon won't happen until January 2018, so make good use of this day. Do something you have never done before, try a new food, go to a movie you otherwise wouldn't dream of watching, or talk to people whose views are very different from yours.

—Magenta Griffith

---

1 Saturday

3rd ♒
☽ v/c 6:02 pm
☽ enters ♓ 6:36 pm
Color: Brown

Lammas/Lughnasadh

---

2 Sunday

3rd ♓
♄ D 1:53 am
Color: Orange

August

3 Monday

3rd ♓
☿ D 7:14 am
☽ v/c 4:35 pm
♃ enters ♑ 7:08 pm
☽ enters ♈ 7:24 pm
Color: Silver

Eucalyptus drives away human and other pests

4 Tuesday

3rd ♈
Color: White

5 Wednesday

3rd ♈
☽ v/c 7:29 pm
☽ enters ♉ 9:29 pm
Color: Yellow

Celtic Tree Month of Hazel begins

◗ Thursday

3rd ♉
4th quarter 10:03 pm
Color: Crimson

7 Friday

4th ♉
☿ enters ♍ 3:15 pm
Color: Purple

Lammas crossquarter day
(Sun reaches 15° Leo)

Set in Eastern Daylight Time (EDT)

Jasmine

With a delicious, sensuality-awakening scent that arrives in the warmer months and increases after dark (in India, some call her "Queen of the Night"), jasmine confers the feeling that all is well, within and without. Magically speaking, she brings peace and happiness to the heart, opens us up to romantic love, and tunes us in to prosperity. Jasmine incense or jasmine absolute can enhance spells, rituals, and intentions related to beauty, attraction, sensuality, sexual healing, love, stress relief, happiness, and prosperity. Jasmine's soothing and stress-relieving qualities also lend themselves to physical healing. To lift your spirits with a potent joy potion, brew a cup of jasmine green tea mixed with dried rose petals. Add 4 drops of jasmine essence, and slowly drink. For an alcoholic version, add 4 drops of jasmine essence to a glass of pink champagne. For a night of irresistibility, light a pink or white candle and a stick of jasmine incense in the bathroom. Draw a warm bath and add a few drops of jasmine absolute and a cup of sea salt. Invoke Archangel Jophiel, the angel of beauty, and request that she infuse the water with the energies of beauty and charm. Soak for at least 30 minutes.

—Tess Whitehurst

---

8 Saturday

4th ♉
☽ v/c 12:46 am
☽ enters ♊ 1:40 am
♂ enters ♌ 7:32 pm
Color: Black

---

9 Sunday

4th ♊
Color: Yellow

A forked hazel branch can divine not only the location of water, but also truth or falsehood

---

August

10 Monday

4th ♊
☽ v/c 7:45 am
☽ enters ♋ 8:08 am
Color: Lavender

11 Tuesday

4th ♋
♃ enters ♍ 7:11 am
Color: Black

Saraphinite promotes compassion and healing

12 Wednesday

4th ♋
♆ ℞ 2:02 am
☽ v/c 1:44 pm
☽ enters ♌ 4:52 pm
Color: White

Gurzil is the Libyan god of the sun, and also war

13 Thursday

4th ♌
Color: Green

☽ Friday

4th ♌
New Moon 10:53 am
Color: Pink

Set in Eastern Daylight Time (EDT)

15 Saturday

1st ♌
☽ v/c 12:36 am
☽ enters ♍ 3:46 am
Color: Blue

Tatjenen is an Egyptian earth god from the area of Memphis

16 Sunday

1st ♍
Color: Gold

Asteroid Hygeia deals with health

August

17 Monday
1st ♍
☽ v/c 1:16 pm
☽ enters ♎ 4:23 pm
Color: Ivory

Arohiohi is the Maori goddess of mirages

18 Tuesday
1st ♎
Color: Scarlet

19 Wednesday
1st ♎
☽ v/c 10:56 pm
Color: Brown

20 Thursday
1st ♎
☽ enters ♏ 5:24 am
Color: Turquoise

Shiva mudra: place both open hands in lap,
one cupping the other, to receive divine guidance

21 Friday
1st ♏
Color: White

Set in Eastern Daylight Time (EDT)

Crepe (or Crape) Myrtle

At first glance, crepe myrtle appears delicate, when in fact her resilience is legendary: her blossoms remain attractive through long summers—even in record heat. This mirrors her magical properties and uses, namely enduring partnerships, continued inspiration (vs. "burnout"), youthfulness, and graceful aging. To bless a new home that you're sharing with a partner and to fill it with vibes conducive to a harmonious long-term relationship, mist with rose water into which you've added 5 drops crepe myrtle essence and 15 drops of neroli essential oil. You might use the leftovers at times to mist yourself and your partner after an argument or help you emotionally connect. To use it as a personal "fountain of youth" potion—just lightly mist your face and body. A few drops of crepe myrtle essence under the tongue can be just the thing anytime you're undergoing a major life shift, such as a change in residence, job change, or after the birth or death of a loved one. Similarly, you can use the blossoms or essence in spells related to moving gracefully through change. Crepe myrtle is also great for calming the mind and connecting us with the underlying stillness that is at the heart of everything.

—Tess Whitehurst

☽ Saturday

1st ♏
☽ v/c 3:31 pm
2nd quarter 3:31 pm
☽ enters ♐ 4:41 pm
Color: Gray

Wear blue for patience and fertility

---

23 Sunday

2nd ♐
☉ enters ♍ 6:37 am
Color: Amber

Sun enters Virgo

24 Monday
2nd ♐
☽ v/c 6:04 pm
Color: White

25 Tuesday
2nd ♐
☽ enters ♑ 12:22 am
Color: Gray

Carrry kyanite for creativity and communication

26 Wednesday
2nd ♑
Color: Topaz

*Jar'Edo Wens, an Australian god
of earthly knowledge, ensures that
humans do not get too arrogant*

27 Thursday
2nd ♑
☽ v/c 3:20 am
☽ enters ♒ 4:03 am
☿ enters ♎ 11:44 am
Color: Purple

Petunias say, "Your presence soothes me"

28 Friday
2nd ♒
Color: Rose

Hungry Ghost Festival (China)

Today is the Ghost Festival, also known as the Hungry Ghost Festival, or Yu Lan. It is a traditional Chinese holiday celebrated in many countries. With roots in Buddhism, the Hungry Ghost Festival is a time of honoring ancestors and appeasing the "hungry ghosts" that wander the world of the living when the "Gates of Hell" are opened this one day a year. To appease these lost souls and to prevent them from harming the living, people put food out for the ghosts to enjoy. Elaborate ceremonies and rituals are also performed to please the ghosts. Activities such as swimming and traveling are avoided because a malicious ghost might cause an accident. Getting married and moving are also avoided, since it is considered an unlucky time.

In certain ways, this is the Chinese equivalent of Samhain, or Dia de los Muertos. The passage to the afterlife is open, whether one calls it the Gates of Hell, or the veil between the worlds. People leave food for those who have died, and visit places of burial. If you can, visit the graves of ancestors or loved ones.

—Magenta Griffith

☺ **Saturday**

2nd ≈
☽ v/c 3:03 am
☽ enters ♓ 4:51 am
Full Moon 2:35 pm
Color: Black

Corn Moon

---

30 Sunday

3rd ♓
Color: Yellow

---

31 Monday

3rd ♓
☽ v/c 2:53 am
☽ enters ♈ 4:33 am
Color: Gray

1 Tuesday

3rd ♈
☽ v/c 12:37 pm
Color: Red

*Prithvi mudra: touch the tips of the
thumb and ring finger to release irrationality*

2 Wednesday

3rd ♈
☽ enters ♉ 5:02 am
Color: White

Celtic Tree Month of Vine begins

3 Thursday

3rd ♉
Color: Turquoise

4 Friday

3rd ♉
☽ v/c 6:20 am
☽ enters ♊ 7:48 am
Color: Pink

Irish moss promotes a steady flow of money

◑ **Saturday**

3rd ♊
4th quarter 5:54 am
☽ v/c 7:04 pm
Color: Gray

Call to your perfect lover by writing desired
traits on the Lovers card from the Tarot

6 **Sunday**

4th ♊
♀ D 4:29 am
☽ enters ♋ 1:40 pm
Color: Gold

September

7 Monday
4th ♋
Color: White

Labor Day

8 Tuesday
4th ♋
☽ v/c 9:28 pm
☽ enters ♌ 10:36 pm
Color: Gray

9 Wednesday
4th ♌
Color: Yellow

*Asteroid Urania indicates where a person excels
in theoretical knowledge or managing information*

10 Thursday
4th ♌
Color: Crimson

11 Friday
4th ♌
☽ v/c 9:03 am
☽ enters ♍ 9:56 am
Color: Rose

Pray to Anat, the Syrian goddess of war, for victory in conflicts

Set in Eastern Daylight Time (EDT)

Carrot Curry Soup

*2–5 large carrots or one package
   of baby carrots.
1–2 cups water
1 bouillon cube
1 T. curry
1 T. turmeric
1 tsp. chili powder
1 T. lemon juice
Raisins, stewed tomatoes (optional)

Peel the carrots if desired, and slice
into small pieces if necessary. Place
in crockpot or stew pan. Dissolve
the bouillon cube in the water and add the spices and lemon juice. Cook
carrots until tender. Turn off heat. Either using an immersion blender or
a stand blender, puree the ingredients until they form a chowderlike con-
sistency. Serve warm, garnished with raisins or stewed tomatoes if desired.

*Peeling is optional: while the peel was once widely believed to be
toxic, research has shown that root vegetable peels are not dangerous to
people of average sensitivities.

Carrots can be harvested right up until the first frost. Their orange color
reminds us of fall, and their association with soil honors the sacrificial God.

—Diana Rajchel

12 Saturday
4th ♍
Color: Blue

*Don't move an old broom into a new
house, to avoid bringing bad luck along*

☽ Sunday
4th ♍
New Moon 2:41 am
☽ v/c 10:08 pm
☽ enters ♎ 10:41 pm
Color: Orange

Solar eclipse 2:54 am, 20° ♍ 12'

September

14 Monday

1st ♎︎
♃ D 3:14 pm
Color: Gray

Rosh Hashanah

15 Tuesday

1st ♎︎
Color: White

16 Wednesday

1st ♎︎
☽ v/c 12:22 am
☽ enters ♏︎ 11:43 am
Color: Topaz

Knotweed is used for binding

17 Thursday

1st ♏︎
♅ enters ♎︎ 5:58 am
☿ R 2:09 pm
♄ enters ♐︎ 10:49 pm
Color: Purple

Mercury retrograde until October 9

18 Friday

1st ♏︎
☽ v/c 3:49 pm
☽ enters ♐︎ 11:32 pm
Color: Coral

Set in Eastern Daylight Time (EDT)

Mabon – Sacrifice and Balance

Mabon, the Autumnal Equinox, is the counterpart to the Spring Equinox. Only on these two days of the year are the day and night exactly equal, in balance. As we celebrate the second of our three harvest festivals, we rejoice in the harvest of apples, corn, squash, and the many other fruits and vegetables that are abundant this time of year. More than that, we rejoice in our own personal harvests—both mundane and magickal.

Back when the light was returning, many of us established goals for the year. Mabon is the perfect time to check in on your progress. Have you harvested everything you'd hoped to during the months in between? If not, what stands in your way, and how can you achieve the balance we all strive for? The Autumnal Equinox is a good time for doing magick for clarity and balance before we head into winter. Now the light is fading, the days grow colder, and we are moving into the darker, colder days of the year. In some traditions, the god sacrifices himself at Mabon for the good of the land— what will you sacrifice for the good of your own spiritual growth?

While you ponder, don't forget to feast on the bounty of the season!

—Deborah Blake

19 Saturday
1st ♐
Color: Black

20 Sunday
1st ♐
Color: Yellow

To find a good job, tie a picture of yourself between two gold coins

◑ Monday

1st ♐
☽ v/c 4:59 am
2nd quarter 4:59 am
☽ enters ♑ 8:33 am
Color: Silver

UN International Day of Peace

22 Tuesday

2nd ♑
☽ v/c 7:13 pm
Color: Maroon

23 Wednesday

2nd ♑
☉ enters ♎ 4:21 am
☽ enters ♒ 1:51 pm
Color: Brown

Yom Kippur
Mabon/Fall Equinox
Sun enters Libra

24 Thursday

2nd ♒
♂ enters ♍ 10:18 pm
Color: White

Lemongrass oil boosts psychic awareness

25 Friday

2nd ♒
☽ v/c 12:02 am
♇ D 2:57 am
☽ enters ♓ 3:43 pm
Color: Purple

Chinese Mooncake Festival

This Full Moon is *zhong qiu jie*, the Chinese Mooncake festival or Mid-Autumn festival. People eat moon cakes—round pastries filled with red bean paste or other ingredients—during the festival. Moon cakes, together with the Full Moon, symbolize happiness and reunion. People tell the story of the moon fairy living in a crystal palace, who comes out to dance on the moon. The legend about the lady living in the moon dates back centuries, to a day when ten suns appeared at once in the sky. The Emperor ordered a famous archer to shoot down the nine extra suns. Once the task was accomplished, the Goddess of Western Heaven rewarded the archer with a pill that would make him immortal. However, his wife found the pill, took it, and was banished to the moon as a result. Legend says that her beauty is greatest on the day of the moon festival. Families get together to look at the Full Moon, feast, eat moon cakes, and sing moon poems. The holiday is similar to Thanksgiving Day in North American countries, a harvest festival.

This would be an auspicious occasion to get together with friends to feast under the Full Moon. End with a round light-colored cake for dessert.

—Magenta Griffith

26 Saturday

2nd ♓
☽ v/c 12:32 pm
Color: Indigo

☺ Sunday

2nd ♓
☽ enters ♈ 3:29 pm
Full Moon 10:51 pm
Color: Amber

Harvest Moon
Lunar eclipse 10:47 pm, 4° ♈ 37'

28 Monday
3rd ♈︎
Color: Ivory

Sukkot begins

29 Tuesday
3rd ♈︎
☽ v/c 3:45 am
☽ enters ♉︎ 2:57 pm
Color: Black

30 Wednesday
3rd ♉︎
Color: White

Celtic Tree Month of Ivy begins

1 Thursday
3rd ♉︎
☽ v/c 6:44 am
☽ enters ♊︎ 4:03 pm
Color: Green

2 Friday
3rd ♊︎
Color: Rose

Purple hyacinth sends a sincere apology

3 Saturday

3rd ♊
☽ v/c 1:18 pm
☽ enters ♋ 8:22 pm
Color: Indigo

Ivy symbolizes death and rebirth

☾ Sunday

3rd ♋
4th quarter 5:06 pm
Color: Amber

Sukkot ends

October

5 Monday

4th ♋
☽ v/c 7:04 am
Color: White

Ninkasi is the Sumerian goddess
of alcoholic beverages, especially beer

6 Tuesday

4th ♋
☽ enters ♌ 4:31 am
Color: Gray

7 Wednesday

4th ♌
☽ v/c 5:10 pm
Color: Yellow

Catch a falling leaf before it touches
the ground, and you may make a wish

8 Thursday

4th ♌
♀ enters ♍ 1:29 pm
☽ enters ♍ 3:50 pm
Color: Purple

9 Friday

4th ♍
☿ D 10:57 am
☽ v/c 6:12 pm
Color: Coral

Burn a pink candle in front of a mirror
to make your image seem more beautiful

Set in Eastern Daylight Time (EDT)

Sunflower

Not only is sunflower named after the sun, his botanical name, *Helianthus*, comes from the Greek god of the sun, Helios. What's more, many anthropologists believe that he was a highly recognizable symbol of the solar deity who appeared in a number of guises throughout Central and South America. Potently aligned with the sun, this flower can be employed in sun magic, and magic for expansion, happiness, health, vitality, sustenance,  radiance, and strength. Create a solar-mist potion by floating a sunflower blossom on top of a glass bowl of pure water in bright sunlight for 15 minutes to an hour. Place the water in a mister (pour the rest of it along with the blossom at the base of a tree). Add 3 drops each of tangerine and neroli essential oil. Shake well and then mist your space to activate happiness and joy. For reliable prosperity and to protect against poverty, dry the blossoms from one sunflower and place them in a red flannel charm bag with a citrine quartz and 4 unshelled sunflower seeds. Tie closed and keep in your kitchen. To enhance health and vitality or to activate confidence and personal power, take 2 to 3 drops of the flower essence under the tongue.

—Tess Whitehurst

---

10 Saturday
4th ♍
Color: Black

Opal initiates spontaneity and female passion

---

11 Sunday
4th ♍
☽ enters ♎ 4:45 am
Color: Yellow

October

☽ Monday
4th ♎︎
☽ v/c 8:06 pm
New Moon 8:06 pm
Color: Silver

Columbus Day (observed)

13 Tuesday
1st ♎︎
☽ enters ♏︎ 5:38 pm
Color: Scarlet

14 Wednesday
1st ♏︎
☽ v/c 8:58 pm
Color: Brown

Islamic New Year

15 Thursday
1st ♏︎
Color: Green

16 Friday
1st ♏︎
☽ enters ♐︎ 5:18 am
Color: White

Asteroid Atropos pinpoints endings and beginnings

Sauerkraut Proper

Harvest season is also preservation season, as we prepare food for winter storage through freezing, pickling, drying, and canning. Sauerkraut is pickled cabbage—and to Slavic folks, a harbinger of coming winter.

1 can (8 oz.) sauerkraut (Frank's brand works well with this recipe)
1 T. olive oil or butter
1 small onion, chopped
3 cloves garlic, minced
1–2 apples, sliced, cored, and chopped
1 cucumber, chopped (optional)
Caraway seeds or celery seeds

Drain the sauerkraut in a colander. Rinse with water two or three times, pounding the liquid out with a wooden spoon. In a frying pan, use the oil or butter to sauté the onions and garlic. Add the sauerkraut just as the onions appear clear. Lightly brown the kraut. Scrape the kraut, onions, garlic, and liquid into a baking dish. Add the apples and cucumbers. Stir thoroughly. Sprinkle caraway and/or celery seeds on top. Serve warm.

—Diana Rajchel

17 Saturday

1st ♐
Color: Blue

Apaan mudra: touch the tips of your middle two fingers and thumb to flush out toxins

18 Sunday

1st ♐
☽ v/c 4:48 am
☽ enters ♑ 2:52 pm
Color: Orange

October

19 Monday
1st ♑
Color: Lavender

A bow made of yew strikes true,
and the faithful hunter will
never return home empty-handed

◐ Tuesday
1st ♑
☽ v/c 4:31 pm
2nd quarter 4:31 pm
☽ enters ♒ 9:38 pm
Color: White

21 Wednesday
2nd ♒
Color: White

Do not give a knife as a housewarming gift,
lest the new neighbor become an enemy

22 Thursday
2nd ♒
Color: Turquoise

23 Friday
2nd ♒
☽ v/c 12:22 am
☽ enters ♓ 1:18 am
☉ enters ♏ 1:47 pm
Color: Pink

Sun enters Scorpio

Set in Eastern Daylight Time (EDT)

Samhain – Endings and Beginnings

The third and final harvest festival, also known as "The Witches' New Year," celebrates both the end of the old year and the beginning of the new. On this day, the veil between the world is at its thinnest, and so we use this time to speak to those who have come before us: our ancestors, our beloved dead, all who are no longer with us. Some celebrate with a Dumb Supper, a traditional meal eaten in complete silence, with plates set out for those  we have lost. Others set up a special altar with candles honoring the dead, often decorated with pictures or tokens to represent each individual. Some use this night for divination, which is enhanced as the veil is thin.

This is a bittersweet holiday when we say goodbye to those we've lost in the year gone past as well as mourn whatever goals we didn't achieve. But it is also a celebration of the coming year, full of hope and anticipation. We wipe the slate clean, dancing around a bonfire in celebration of the Goddess in her Crone persona; full of wisdom and ready to sustain us as we move into the darkness of winter. She teaches us that the dark is nothing to fear, only a quiet place where we can rest until we are ready to begin again.

—Deborah Blake

24 Saturday

2nd ♓
☽ v/c 7:18 am
Color: Gray

Selkis, the Egyptian scorpion goddess, protects the places of the dead from encroachment by the living

25 Sunday

2nd ♓
☽ enters ♈ 2:22 am
♆ enters ♓ 6:01 am
Color: Gold

Yellow supports learning, concentration, and memory

26 Monday
2nd ♈
☽ v/c 8:25 am
Color: Gray

☻ Tuesday
2nd ♈
☽ enters ♉ 2:07 am
Full Moon 8:05 am
♃ enters ♒ 11:56 am
Color: Red

Blood Moon

28 Wednesday
3rd ♉
☽ v/c 11:20 am
Color: Topaz

Celtic Tree Month of Reed begins

29 Thursday
3rd ♉
☽ enters ♊ 2:24 am
Color: Crimson

Llyr is the Welsh god of the sea and fishing

30 Friday
3rd ♊
☽ v/c 10:52 pm
Color: White

Otsukimi (Japan)

Otsukimi, literally "moon-view-ing," is the Japanese festival honoring the October Full Moon. Offerings include unripe soybeans (edamame) and chestnuts, both of which are round like the moon. In China, it is called "The Kindly Moon." September Full Moon viewing is common to both China and Japan, but October Full Moon viewing is unique to Japan. A tenth-century emperor and his courtiers decided that they liked the October

Full Moon as well and the tradition began. People eat dumplings, which are round and white like the moon, that are decorated with Japanese susuki grass, a common symbol of autumn. Festivals dedicated to the moon have a long history in Japan. Members of the aristocratic class would hold moon-viewing events aboard boats in order to view the moon's reflection on the surface of the water.

This is an excellent night to gather with friends to look at the beauty of the Full Moon, especially if you can go to a place where you can see the moon reflected in water, such as a lake.

—Magenta Griffith

31 Saturday

3rd ♊
☽ enters ♋ 5:09 am
♀ enters ♑ 7:07 am
Color: Brown

Samhain/Halloween

1 Sunday

3rd ♋
☽ v/c 10:35 pm
Color: Orange

All Saints' Day
Daylight Saving Time ends at 2 am

November

2 Monday
3rd ♋
☿ enters ♏ 2:06 am
☽ enters ♌ 10:48 am
Color: White

Use a quartz crystal to write your desire into the side of a candle

○ Tuesday
3rd ♌
4th quarter 7:24 am
☽ v/c 8:46 pm
Color: Black

Election Day (general)

4 Wednesday
4th ♌
☽ enters ♍ 9:22 pm
Color: Brown

5 Thursday
4th ♍
Color: Green

Oil of sage keeps memory strong and promotes wisdom

6 Friday
4th ♍
Color: Purple

Set in Eastern Standard Time (EDT)

Marigold (Tagetes)

What Dia de los Muertos celebration would be complete without marigold (the tagetes variety, or "common marigold," rather than calendula)? Appearing on elaborate altars to the deceased, marigold shines, paying homage to the deceased one's memory and his/her aliveness in the spirit realm. Indeed, marigold is revered for his ability to lend movement and vitality to the cycle of death and rebirth, to comfort the living by reminding us of

natural cycles, and to enhance communication between the physical and spiritual realms. Marigold helps bring us into alignment with our natural state of happiness, especially as the days get colder and the nights get longer. As such, he can be an excellent addition to a holiday centerpiece or any working related to happiness and joy. In fact, the flower essence can be an effective medicine for or seasonal affective disorder. In *The Encyclopedia of Magical Herbs*, Scott Cunningham writes, "Marigolds, picked at noon when the sun is at its hottest and strongest, will strengthen and comfort the heart." Additionally, marigold can be a helpful ally for things like job interviews and court cases, as his vital, fortifying energy can act as a magical success tonic.

—Tess Whitehurst

7 Saturday
4th ♍
☽ v/c 7:47 am
☽ enters ♎ 10:14 am
Color: Blue

8 Sunday
4th ♎
♀ enters ♎ 10:31 am
☽ v/c 9:42 pm
Color: Amber

Samhain crossquarter day
(Sun reaches 15° Scorpio)

November

9 Monday
4th ♎︎
☽ enters ♏︎ 11:02 pm
Color: Gray

The Hindu goddess Matangi relates
to the throat chakra and divine speech

10 Tuesday
4th ♎︎
Color: Maroon

🌑 Wednesday
4th ♏︎
New Moon 12:47 pm
Color: Topaz

Veterans Day

12 Thursday
1st ♏︎
☽ v/c 9:54 am
☽ enters ♐︎ 10:14 am
♂ enters ♎︎ 4:41 pm
Color: White

13 Friday
1st ♐︎
⚳ D 1:09 pm
☽ v/c 10:19 pm
Color: Rose

Bestow a crown of roses to recognize merit

14 Saturday
1st ♐
☽ enters ♑ 7:21 pm
Color: Brown

Asteroid Hecate hints at psychic power or deep
spirituality, but rarely gives a straight answer

15 Sunday
1st ♑
Color: Gold

November

16 Monday
1st ♑
☽ v/c 3:53 pm
Color: Lavender

17 Tuesday
1st ♑
☽ enters ♒ 2:24 am
Color: White

Master root enhances power

18 Wednesday
1st ♒
♆ D 11:31 am
Color: Yellow

☽ Thursday

1st ♒
2nd quarter 1:27 am
☽ v/c 3:19 am
☽ enters ♓ 7:21 am
Color: Crimson

Use a chalice when working spells with the divine feminine

20 Friday

2nd ♓
☿ enters ♐ 2:43 pm
Color: Coral

Set in Eastern Standard Time (EST)

Chrysanthemum

When the light wanes and the days grow shorter, chrysanthemum knows that it's his cue to bloom. In fact, all of chrysanthemum's magical properties have to do with shining light into darkness or shoring up one's strength at a time it might naturally diminish. What's more, as all alchemists know, *chrysos* (Greek for "gold") represents the energy of the sun and all its life-giving, life-sustaining attributes. Longevity is perhaps chrysanthemum's specialty:

he not only helps us to live a long life, but to do so with strength and vigor. For this purpose, take the flower essence, plant mums in your yard, or ceremonially brew and drink tea made with a dried chrysanthemum blossom. Chrysanthemum is also a great magical ingredient for dissolving muddleheadedness, confusion, or mystery in the light of clarity and understanding. For clarity, you might want to spend time in quiet contemplation with a chrysanthemum blossom. Relax and allow yourself to open to the flower's silent wisdom. Similarly, chrysanthemum is an expert at protecting us from invisible dangers such as earthbound entities or psychic attack. For these concerns, simply carrying a fresh blossom can help.

—Tess Whitehurst

21 Saturday
2nd ♓
☽ v/c 8:23 am
☽ enters ♈ 10:12 am
Color: Gray

If you give shoes as a gift, the recipient will walk out of your life

22 Sunday
2nd ♈
☉ enters ♐ 10:25 am
☽ v/c 2:16 pm
Color: Yellow

Sun enters Sagittarius

November

23 Monday
2nd ♈
☽ enters ♉ 11:26 am
Color: White

Oregano discourages annoying in-laws from causing trouble

24 Tuesday
2nd ♉
☽ v/c 8:26 pm
Color: Gray

☺ Wednesday
2nd ♉
☽ enters ♊ 12:15 pm
Full Moon 5:44 pm
Color: White

Mourning Moon
Celtic Tree Month of Elder begins

26 Thursday
3rd ♊
☽ v/c 10:35 pm
Color: Purple

Thanksgiving Day

27 Friday
3rd ♊
☽ enters ♋ 2:27 pm
Color: Pink

Loy Krathong (Thai)

In Thailand and nearby areas of Laos and Burma, this Full Moon is Loy Krathong, which means "Floating Decoration" and comes from the tradition of making offerings to rivers. The krathong is an offering made of elaborately folded banana leaves (or spider lilies), incense sticks, and a candle; a small coin is sometimes included. On this Full Moon, Thais make a wish and launch their krathong on a river, canal, or a pond, as the festival comes from an ancient ritual paying respect to the water spirits. To celebrate Loy Krathong, carry a krathong to the water when the sun goes down and ask the water spirits to take their ill-fortune, troubles, and pain away. They light candles inside the krathongs to help the boats find their way. People release the krathongs into the water and watch as they float away. In some communities, people linger around the water and share conversation, food, or drinks with their neighbors. In Bangkok and other big cities, fireworks go off at midnight to end the celebration. If you live near a body of water, this would be a good night to make an offering, flowers, food, or other biodegradable items.

—Magenta Griffith

28 Saturday

3rd ♋
☿ D 1:43 am
Color: Black

29 Sunday

3rd ♋
☽ v/c 7:46 am
☽ enters ♌ 7:47 pm
Color: Orange

*Shunya mudra: fold the middle finger
completely under the thumb to
reduce motion sickness or vertigo*

30 Monday
3rd ♌
Color: Ivory

A bouquet of withered flowers is a rejection of a suitor's attention

1 Tuesday
3rd ♌
☽ v/c 10:09 pm
Color: Scarlet

2 Wednesday
3rd ♌
☽ enters ♍ 5:09 am
Color: White

Iolite boosts psychic ability and spiritual growth

◑ Thursday
3rd ♍
4th quarter 2:40 am
⚶ enters ♈ 12:58 pm
☽ v/c 11:59 pm
Color: Turquoise

4 Friday
4th ♍
☽ enters ♎ 5:34 pm
♀ enters ♏ 11:15 pm
Color: Rose

5 Saturday
4th ♎︎
Color: Brown

6 Sunday
4th ♎︎
☽ v/c 9:03 pm
Color: Amber

To reduce anger, hold a rock and visualize the
anger flowing into it; then throw the rock away

December

7 Monday
4th ♎
☽ enters ♏ 6:26 am
Color: White

Hanukkah begins

8 Tuesday
4th ♏
Color: Black

9 Wednesday
4th ♏
☽ v/c 1:39 am
☽ enters ♐ 5:25 pm
☿ enters ♑ 9:34 pm
Color: Yellow

Oil of marjoram soothes sexual urges

10 Thursday
4th ♐
✳ enters ♏ 2:50 am
Color: Purple

☽ Friday
4th ♐
New Moon 5:29 am
☽ v/c 11:06 am
Color: Pink

Purple conveys wisdom, age, and spiritual power

Set in Eastern Standard Time (EST)

Popovers

Tasty and versatile, popovers are a uniquely North American dish, descended from British Yorkshire pudding. At a time we see the sun the least, we rely on comfort foods to nourish us.

3 beaten eggs
1 cup milk
2 T. melted butter
½ tsp. salt
1 tsp. sugar
1 cup flour

Preheat oven to 450 degrees F. Grease popover tins (or muffin tins) or line with silicone cups. Beat together eggs, milk, butter, salt, and sugar. Beat in flour until smooth. Fill the tins halfway with batter. Place in oven for 15 minutes, then reduce heat to 350 degrees F, and bake for another 15 to 20 minutes. Do NOT open oven during baking. Remove from oven when they are light brown and fluffy. Allow to cool until they are warm enough to touch. Top with berries and jam if served as a dessert. Popovers are an excellent breakfast dish to enjoy as a holiday morning tradition along with bacon, eggs, and jam, which should tide you over until the late-afternoon feast.

—Diana Rajchel

12 Saturday

1st ♐
☽ enters ♑ 1:46 am
Color: Gray

Asteroid Fortuna speaks of a person's approach to luck, good or bad

13 Sunday

1st ♑
☽ v/c 6:07 pm
Color: Yellow

December

14 Monday

1st ♑︎
☽ enters ♒︎ 7:59 am
Color: Gray

Hanukkah ends

15 Tuesday

1st ♒︎
Color: Red

Tannit is the Libyan goddess of weaving and other fibercrafts

16 Wednesday

1st ♒︎
☽ v/c 2:17 am
☽ enters ♓︎ 12:45 pm
Color: Brown

17 Thursday

1st ♓︎
Color: White

Tie a knot in a handkerchief to ward off evil

☽ Friday

1st ♓︎
☽ v/c 10:14 am
2nd quarter 10:14 am
☽ enters ♈︎ 4:26 pm
Color: Purple

Set in Eastern Standard Time (EST)

Yule – Celebrate the Solstice

Yule, or the Winter Solstice, a day celebrated around the world as a beacon of light in the midst of darkness. Yule is the longest night of the year, and for many, the winter has come bringing short days with plenty of cold and not enough light. Yet the solstice is a day of hope, because after this, the sun begins its slow return, increasing more with every day until the wheel of the year turns, bringing us around to spring again.

The Goddess is now in her Mother persona, having given birth to the infant god and completing the cycle of birth, growth, death, and rebirth. The Oak King has battled his brother the Holly King and won back his scepter, and so the waxing portion of the year begins again.

Many familiar Christmas traditions came from this holiday (listen to carolers sing of "Yuletide merry"), making this the perfect holiday to share with Pagan and non-Pagan friends and family. The fir tree and evergreen boughs represent life in the midst of death, because they survive when most plants die. So decorate your tree with magickal symbols and raise a cup of mulled cider to the newborn Sun. May the light ever be with you!

—Deborah Blake

---

19 Saturday
2nd ♈
Color: Black

---

20 Sunday
2nd ♈
☽ v/c 5:01 pm
☽ enters ♉ 7:13 pm
Color: Gold

Yerba santa is placed on altars as an offering

December

21 Monday

2nd ♉
☉ enters ♑ 11:48 pm
Color: Silver

Yule/Winter Solstice
Sun enters Capricorn

22 Tuesday

2nd ♉
☽ v/c 9:26 am
☽ enters ♊ 9:31 pm
Color: White

Celtic Tree Month of Elder ends

23 Wednesday

2nd ♊
Color: Topaz

Between (Celtic Tree Month)

24 Thursday

2nd ♊
☽ v/c 3:04 pm
Color: Green

Christmas Eve
Celtic Tree Month of Birch begins

☺ Friday

2nd ♊
☽ enters ♋ 12:27 am
Full Moon 6:12 am
♅ D 10:53 pm
Color: White

Christmas Day
Long Nights Moon

Unduvap (Sri Lanka)

This Full Moon is Unduvap, which celebrates the arrival of the Bo tree sapling in Sri Lanka, and also the transmission of Buddhism to that island. It was brought there from India in 288 BCE by Buddhist nun, Sanghamitta Theri. This bo tree, the oldest tree in existence whose specific planting was documented, is a large fig tree (*Ficus religiosa*) located in India, under which the Buddha is said to have achieved enlightenment, or Bodhi; and this tree

is known to be an offshoot. Later, there were many saplings planted in Sri Lanka, from this Bo-Tree. Theri also established the Bhikkhuni Sasana (the Order of Nuns). Adherents commonly go to temples to chant and pray, and if they can, make a pilgrimage to venerate the bodhi tree.

Many Pagans worship trees in some way. If you can visit a really old tree, it would be worthwhile. What is the oldest tree near your home? Some of the oldest trees are sequoia, bristlecone pine, redwoods, olive trees, cypress, yew, and of course, the sacred fig or bo tree. And of course, this is a perfect day to decorate a tree in your own home or appreciate one that has already been decorated. Spruce and pine are traditional.

—Magenta Griffith

---

26 Saturday

3rd ♋
☽ v/c 10:36 pm
Color: Indigo

Kwanzaa begins

---

27 Sunday

3rd ♋
☽ enters ♌ 5:31 am
Color: Orange

A rod or broom of birch will expel evil spirits

28 Monday
3rd ♌
Color: Lavender

Emerald brings success in business

29 Tuesday
3rd ♌
☽ v/c 12:38 pm
☽ enters ♍ 1:58 pm
Color: Black

Anise oil aids clairvoyance

30 Wednesday
3rd ♍
♀ enters ♐ 2:16 am
Color: White

31 Thursday
3rd ♍
Color: Crimson

New Year's Eve

1 Friday
3rd ♍
☽ v/c 12:33 am
☽ enters ♎ 1:41 am
☿ enters ♒ 9:20 pm
Color: Rose

New Year's Day
Kwanzaa ends

Oak Blossom

Oak gets a lot of press, but not often for his unassuming little blossom. Still, his blossom has quite an impressive resume of metaphysical abilities. For example, he can help us shore up the initiative and perseverance needed to earn money in a long-term, desirable way. To release money worries, conjure up a prosperous mind-set, and magnetize wealth, you might lovingly gather an oak blossom at the New Moon (leaving a silver dollar or shiny dime as a token of gratitude near the base of the tree). Wrap it in a dollar bill, and again in a piece of green cloth, tying it closed with hemp twine. Hold it in both hands and say: "I earn and receive all that I need. I am divinely and perfectly wealthy." Keep it on your altar for one moon cycle and then bury at the base of the same tree. Oak blossom is also a wonderful ally when it comes to procuring sustainable employment. While job hunting, you might gently gather a few oak blossoms and place them on your altar along with a piece of sodalite and a piece of hematite. Say, "My perfect new position is now mine, swiftly, easily, and perfectly. Blessed be." Other intentions related to oak include luck, clarity, focus, energy, and success in school or work.

—Tess Whitehurst

2 Saturday
3rd ♎
4th quarter 12:30 am
☽ v/c 11:23 am
Color: Blue

3 Sunday
4th ♎
♂ enters ♏ 9:32 am
☽ enters ♏ 2:36 pm
Color: Amber

About the Authors

ELIZABETH BARRETTE was the managing editor of *PanGaia* and has been involved with the Pagan community for twenty-four years, actively networking via coffeehouse meetings and open sabbats. Her other writings include speculative fiction and gender studies. Her 2011 poem "The Cathedral of the Michaelangelines" earned a nomination for the Rhysling Award. She lives in central Illinois and enjoys herbal landscaping and gardening for wildlife.

DEBORAH BLAKE is the author of six books on witchcraft from Llewellyn, including *The Goddess is in the Details*, *Everyday Witch A to Z Spellbook*, *Witchcraft on a Shoestring*, and *Everyday Witch Book of Rituals*. She has published numerous articles in Pagan publications, including many Llewellyn annuals, and has a regular column in *Witches & Pagans* magazine. She lives in upstate New York in a 110-year-old farmhouse with her frequent co-author, Magic the Cat, and four other feline overlords. She can be found online at www.deborahblakehps.com, as well as Twitter, Facebook, and her blog.

Life is what you make it, and DALLAS JENNIFER COBB has made a magical life in a waterfront village on the shores of great Lake Ontario. Forever scheming novel ways to pay the bills, she practices manifestation magic and wildlands witchcraft. She teaches Pilates, works in a library, is an elected official and writes to finance long hours spent following her heart's desire—time spent in nature, and on the water. She lives with her daughter and three cats. Contact her at jennifer.cobb@live.com.

KATHLEEN EDWARDS sold her first artworks in sixth grade—drawings of peace signs and flowers for ten cents each. She's been a book illustrator since 1991, including many Llewellyn publications. Her award-winning fine-art paintings have been widely exhibited and her graphic book, *Holy Stars: Favorite Deities, Prophets, Saints and Sages from Around the World* was published in 2009. See more of her work at kathleenedwardsartist.com.

SYBIL FOGG has been a practicing witch for over twenty- five years. Her real name is Sybil Wilen, but she chose to use her mother's maiden name in pagan circles to honor her grandparents. She's also a wife, mother, writer, teacher, and belly dancer. Her family shares her passion for magic, dance, and writing. She lives in Saco, Maine, with her husband and children. Please visit her website: www.sybilwilen.com.

MAGENTA GRIFFITH has been a Witch for more than thirty years and a High Priestess for more than twenty. She is a founding member of the coven Prodea, which has been celebrating rituals since 1980, as well as being a member of various Pagan organizations such as Covenant of the Goddess. She presents classes and workshops at a variety of events around the Midwest. She shares her home with a small black cat and a large collection of books.

MELANIE MARQUIS is a lifelong practitioner of magick, the founder of United Witches global coven, and the author of *The Witch's Bag of Tricks* (Llewellyn, 2011). An eclectic folk witch, mother, tarot reader, environmentalist, and folk artist, she enjoys a busy life enriched with personalized magick and practical spirituality. Visit her online at www.melaniemarquis.com or www.unitedwitches.org.

DIANA RAJCHEL lives in Minneapolis with her husband and sundry robots. She is the author of the book *Divorcing a Real Witch* and the executive editor for the Pagan Newswire Collective. To learn more about her thoughts on contemporary living and more, visit http://blog.dianarajchel.com.

SUZANNE RESS has been writing nonfiction and fiction for many years. She published her first novel, *The Trial of Goody Gilbert*, in 2012, and is currently working on her third. She is an accomplished self-taught gardener, beekeeper, silversmith, and mosaicist. She lives in the woods at the foot of the Alps in northern Italy with her husband, daughter, two dogs, three horses, and an elusive red stag.

TESS WHITEHURST is the author of several books including *Magical Fashionista, Magical Housekeeping, The Magic of Flowers*, and the IPPY award-winning *Good Energy Book*. Her work has been translated into nine languages and her articles have appeared such places as *Law of Attraction Magazine, Whole Life Times*, and *Writer's Digest*. Her blog (enchantingtheday.blogspot.com) and free monthly newsletter (Good Energy) feature simple rituals, meditations, and musings for everyday magical living. She practices feng shui professionally in Los Angeles, where she lives with her boyfriend and their two magical cats.

Appendix

Daily Magical Influences

Each day is ruled by a planet with specific magical influences.

Monday (Moon): peace, healing, caring, psychic awareness
Tuesday (Mars): passion, courage, aggression, protection
Wednesday (Mercury): study, travel, divination, wisdom
Thursday (Jupiter): expansion, money, prosperity, generosity
Friday (Venus): love, friendship, reconciliation, beauty
Saturday (Saturn): longevity, endings, homes
Sunday (Sun): healing, spirituality, success, strength, protection

Color Correspondences

Colors are associated with each day, according to planetary influence.

Monday: gray, lavender, white, silver, ivory
Tuesday: red, white, black, gray, maroon, scarlet
Wednesday: yellow, brown, white, topaz
Thursday: green, turquoise, white, purple, crimson
Friday: white, pink, rose, purple, coral
Saturday: brown, gray, blue, indigo, black
Sunday: yellow, orange, gold, amber

Lunar Phases

Waxing, from New Moon to Full Moon, is the ideal time to do magic to draw things to you.

Waning, from Full Moon to New Moon, is a time for study, meditation, and magical work designed to banish harmful energies.

The Moon's Sign

The Moon continuously moves through each sign of the zodiac, from Aries to Pisces, staying about two and a half days in each sign. The Moon influences the sign it inhabits, creating different energies that affect our day-to-day lives.

Aries: Good for starting things. Things occur rapidly, but quickly pass. People tend to be argumentative and assertive.

Taurus: Things begun now last longest, tend to increase in value, and become hard to change. Brings out an appreciation for beauty and sensory experience.

Gemini: Things begun now are easily changed by outside influence. Time for shortcuts, communication, games, and fun.

Cancer: Stimulates emotional rapport between people. Supports growth and nurturing. Tend to domestic concerns.

Leo: Draws emphasis to the self, to central ideas or institutions, away from connections with others and emotional needs.

Virgo: Favors accomplishment of details and commands from higher up. Focus on health, hygiene, and daily schedules.

Libra: Favors cooperation, compromise, social activities, balance, friendship, and partnership.

Scorpio: Increases awareness of psychic power. Precipitates psychic crises and ends connections thoroughly. People have a tendency to brood and become secretive.

Sagittarius: Encourages confidence and flights of imagination. This is an adventurous, philosophical, and athletic Moon sign. Favors expansion and growth.

Capricorn: Develops strong structure. Focus on traditions, responsibilities, and obligations. A good time to set boundaries and rules.

Aquarius: Rebellious energy. Time to break habits and make abrupt change. Personal freedom and individuality is the focus.

Pisces: The focus is on dreaming, nostalgia, intuition, and psychic impressions. A good time for spiritual or philanthropic activities.

2015 Eclipses

March 20, 5:45 am; Solar eclipse 29° ♓ 29'
April 4, 8:00 am; Lunar eclipse 14° ♎ 21'
September 13, 2:54 am; Solar eclipse 20° ♍ 12'
September 27, 10:47 pm; Lunar eclipse 4° ♈ 37'

2015 Full Moons

Cold Moon: January 4, 11:53 pm
Quickening Moon: February 3, 6:09 pm
Storm Moon: March 5, 1:05 pm
Wind Moon: April 4, 8:06 am
Flower Moon: May 3, 11:42 pm
Strong Sun Moon: June 2, 12:19 pm
Blessing Moon: July 1, 10:20 pm
Blue Moon: July 31, 6:43 am
Corn Moon: August 29, 2:35 pm
Harvest Moon: September 27, 10:51 pm
Blood Moon: October 27, 8:05 am
Mourning Moon: November 25, 5:44 pm
Long Nights Moon: December 25, 6:12 am

Planetary Retrogrades in 2015

Planet		Retrograde			Direct	
Jupiter	℞	12/08/14	3:41 pm	— Direct	04/08/15	12:57 pm
Mercury	℞	01/21/15	10:54 am	— Direct	02/11/15	9:57 am
Saturn	℞	03/14/15	11:02 am	— Direct	08/02/15	1:53 am
Pluto	℞	04/16/15	11:56 pm	— Direct	09/25/15	2:57 am
Mercury	℞	05/18/15	9:49 pm	— Direct	06/11/15	6:33 pm
Neptune	℞	06/12/15	5:09 am	— Direct	11/18/15	11:31 am
Venus	℞	07/25/15	5:29 am	— Direct	09/06/15	4:29 am
Uranus	℞	07/26/15	6:38 am	— Direct	12/25/15	10:53 pm
Mercury	℞	09/17/15	2:09 pm	— Direct	10/09/15	10:57 am

Moon Void-of-Course Data for 2015

JANUARY

Last Aspect Date Time	New Sign Sign New Time
1 7:19 am	1 ♊ 12:09 pm
3 6:55 am	3 ♋ 8:08 pm
4 11:53 pm	6 ♌ 6:03 am
8 12:05 pm	8 ♍ 5:58 pm
10 10:46 am	11 ♎ 6:57 am
13 4:46 am	13 ♏ 6:44 pm
15 6:52 pm	16 ♐ 3:01 am
17 2:25 pm	18 ♑ 7:04 am
19 5:51 am	20 ♒ 7:59 am
21 8:45 pm	22 ♓ 7:48 am
23 6:13 am	24 ♈ 8:31 am
26 9:23 am	26 ♉ 11:37 am
27 9:18 pm	28 ♊ 5:36 pm
30 4:24 am	31 ♋ 2:09 am

FEBRUARY

Last Aspect Date Time	New Sign Sign New Time
1 8:37 am	2 ♌ 12:41 pm
4 12:31 am	5 ♍ 12:46 am
6 5:09 pm	7 ♎ 1:44 pm
9 6:58 am	10 ♏ 2:05 am
12 12:32 am	12 ♐ 11:46 am
14 10:15 am	14 ♑ 5:24 pm
16 3:17 pm	16 ♒ 7:13 pm
18 6:47 pm	18 ♓ 6:47 pm
19 6:02 pm	20 ♈ 6:13 pm
21 7:36 pm	22 ♉ 7:28 pm
23 9:57 pm	24 ♊ 11:54 pm
26 3:43 am	26 ♋ 7:50 am
28 12:53 pm	3/1 ♌ 6:34 pm

MARCH

Last Aspect Date Time	New Sign Sign New Time
2/28 12:53 pm	1 ♌ 6:34 pm
3 3:48 am	4 ♍ 6:58 am
5 1:36 pm	6 ♎ 7:52 pm
8 9:24 pm	9 ♏ 9:10 am
11 3:46 pm	11 ♐ 7:30 pm
13 7:11 pm	14 ♑ 2:40 am
16 4:02 am	16 ♒ 6:14 am
17 2:18 pm	18 ♓ 6:58 am
20 5:36 am	20 ♈ 6:28 am
21 6:51 pm	22 ♉ 6:40 am
23 10:25 am	24 ♊ 9:23 am
26 8:35 am	26 ♋ 3:45 pm
28 9:58 pm	29 ♌ 1:48 am
30 9:57 am	31 ♍ 2:12 pm

APRIL

Last Aspect Date Time	New Sign Sign New Time
2 5:01 am	3 ♎ 3:07 am
4 11:59 am	5 ♏ 3:04 pm
7 4:42 am	8 ♐ 1:08 am
9 1:42 pm	10 ♑ 8:47 am
12 4:15 am	12 ♒ 1:44 pm
14 3:45 pm	14 ♓ 4:12 pm
15 5:37 pm	16 ♈ 5:00 pm
18 2:57 pm	18 ♉ 5:31 pm
19 7:07 pm	20 ♊ 7:28 pm
22 1:38 am	23 ♋ 12:25 am
24 1:04 pm	25 ♌ 9:13 am
27 10:12 am	27 ♍ 9:07 pm
30 8:23 am	30 ♎ 10:03 am

MAY

Last Aspect Date Time	New Sign Sign New Time
2 10:03 am	2 ♏ 9:47 pm
4 9:49 am	5 ♐ 7:13 am
7 1:51 pm	7 ♑ 2:16 pm
9 4:35 pm	9 ♒ 7:22 pm
11 6:36 am	11 ♓ 10:53 pm
13 12:55 pm	14 ♈ 1:13 am
15 8:04 am	16 ♉ 3:02 am
18 12:13 am	18 ♊ 5:27 am
19 1:57 pm	20 ♋ 9:56 am
21 8:36 pm	22 ♌ 5:42 pm
24 6:50 am	25 ♍ 4:52 am
26 10:21 pm	27 ♎ 5:42 pm
29 4:20 pm	30 ♏ 5:34 am

JUNE

Last Aspect Date Time	New Sign Sign New Time
1 7:01 am	1 ♐ 2:39 pm
3 1:59 am	3 ♑ 8:50 pm
5 6:54 am	6 ♒ 1:02 am
7 10:30 am	8 ♓ 4:16 am
9 2:08 pm	10 ♈ 7:14 am
11 7:43 pm	12 ♉ 10:16 am
13 6:06 pm	14 ♊ 1:51 pm
16 10:05 am	16 ♋ 6:51 pm
19 1:52 am	19 ♌ 2:23 am
21 12:09 am	21 ♍ 12:59 pm
24 1:12 am	24 ♎ 1:41 am
25 7:22 pm	26 ♏ 1:57 pm
28 9:50 pm	28 ♐ 11:21 pm
30 2:18 pm	7/1 ♑ 5:11 am

JULY

Last Aspect Date Time	New Sign Sign New Time
6/30 2:18 pm	1 ♑ 5:11 am
3 6:36 am	3 ♒ 8:21 am
5 8:32 am	5 ♓ 10:23 am
7 10:36 am	7 ♈ 12:38 pm
9 9:47 am	9 ♉ 3:49 pm
11 5:52 pm	11 ♊ 8:16 pm
13 11:31 pm	14 ♋ 2:14 am
16 7:24 am	16 ♌ 10:15 am
18 5:41 pm	18 ♍ 8:47 pm
21 6:07 am	21 ♎ 9:23 am
23 2:12 pm	23 ♏ 10:07 pm
26 5:14 am	26 ♐ 8:24 am
28 9:36 am	28 ♑ 2:47 pm
30 2:50 pm	30 ♒ 5:40 pm

AUGUST

Last Aspect Date Time	New Sign Sign New Time
1 6:02 pm	1 ♓ 6:36 pm
3 4:35 pm	3 ♈ 7:24 pm
5 7:29 pm	5 ♉ 9:29 pm
8 12:46 am	8 ♊ 1:40 am
10 7:45 am	10 ♋ 8:08 am
12 1:44 pm	12 ♌ 4:52 pm
15 12:36 am	15 ♍ 3:46 am
17 1:16 pm	17 ♎ 4:23 pm
19 10:56 pm	20 ♏ 5:24 am
22 3:31 pm	22 ♐ 4:41 pm
24 6:04 pm	25 ♑ 12:22 am
27 3:20 am	27 ♒ 4:03 am
29 3:03 am	29 ♓ 4:51 am
31 2:53 am	31 ♈ 4:33 am

SEPTEMBER

Last Aspect Date Time	New Sign Sign New Time
1 12:37 pm	2 ♉ 5:02 am
4 6:20 am	4 ♊ 7:48 am
5 7:04 pm	6 ♋ 1:40 pm
8 9:28 pm	8 ♌ 10:36 pm
11 9:03 am	11 ♍ 9:56 am
13 10:08 pm	13 ♎ 10:41 pm
16 12:22 am	16 ♏ 11:43 am
18 3:49 pm	18 ♐ 11:32 pm
21 4:59 am	21 ♑ 8:33 am
22 7:13 pm	23 ♒ 1:51 pm
25 12:02 am	25 ♓ 3:43 pm
26 12:32 pm	27 ♈ 3:29 pm
29 3:45 am	29 ♉ 2:57 pm

OCTOBER

Last Aspect Date Time	New Sign Sign New Time
1 6:44 am	1 ♊ 4:03 pm
3 1:18 pm	3 ♋ 8:22 pm
5 7:04 am	6 ♌ 4:31 am
7 5:10 pm	8 ♍ 3:50 pm
9 6:12 pm	11 ♎ 4:45 am
12 8:06 pm	13 ♏ 5:38 pm
14 8:58 pm	16 ♐ 5:18 am
18 4:48 am	18 ♑ 2:52 pm
20 4:31 pm	20 ♒ 9:38 pm
23 12:22 am	23 ♓ 1:18 am
24 7:18 am	25 ♈ 2:22 am
26 8:25 am	27 ♉ 2:07 am
28 11:20 pm	29 ♊ 2:24 am
30 10:52 pm	31 ♋ 5:09 am

NOVEMBER

Last Aspect Date Time	New Sign Sign New Time
1 10:35 pm	2 ♌ 10:48 am
3 8:46 pm	4 ♍ 9:22 pm
7 7:47 am	7 ♎ 10:14 am
8 9:42 pm	9 ♏ 11:02 pm
12 9:54 am	12 ♐ 10:14 am
13 10:19 pm	14 ♑ 7:21 pm
16 3:53 pm	17 ♒ 2:34 am
19 3:19 am	19 ♓ 7:21 am
21 8:23 am	21 ♈ 10:12 am
22 2:16 pm	23 ♉ 11:26 am
24 8:26 pm	25 ♊ 12:15 pm
26 10:35 pm	27 ♋ 2:27 pm
29 7:46 pm	29 ♌ 7:47 pm

DECEMBER

Last Aspect Date Time	New Sign Sign New Time
1 10:09 pm	2 ♍ 5:09 am
3 11:59 pm	4 ♎ 5:34 pm
6 9:03 pm	7 ♏ 6:26 am
9 1:39 am	9 ♐ 5:25 pm
11 11:06 am	12 ♑ 1:46 am
13 6:07 pm	14 ♒ 7:59 am
16 2:17 am	16 ♓ 12:45 pm
18 10:14 am	18 ♈ 4:26 pm
20 5:01 pm	20 ♉ 7:13 pm
22 9:26 am	22 ♊ 9:31 pm
24 3:04 pm	25 ♋ 12:27 am
26 10:36 pm	27 ♌ 5:31 am
29 12:38 pm	29 ♍ 1:58 pm

Set in Eastern Time. All times corrected for Daylight Saving Time.

Practical Ways to Augment Your Craft

Llewellyn's *Magical Almanac* has been inspiring all levels of magical practitioners for over twenty years. Filled with practical spells, rituals, and fresh ideas, you'll find new ways to deepen your craft and enhance everyday life.

This edition features compelling articles on plant allies, menopause and magick, using the element of surprise in a ritual, the sacred wells of Ireland, marrying a non-Pagan, organizing a shapeshifting dance, graveyard magick, and more. Also included is a calendar section featuring world festivals, holidays, astrological information, incense and color correspondences, and 2015 Sabbats.

LLEWELLYN'S 2015
MAGICAL ALMANAC
336 pp. • 5¼ x 8
978-0-7387-2685-4 • U.S. $10.99 Can $12.50
To order call 1-877-NEW-WRLD
www.llewellyn.com

Notes

Notes

Notes